THE PRAYING LIFE

Seeking God in All Things

Deborah Smith Douglas

MOREHOUSE PUBLISHING
A Continuum imprint
HARRISBURG • LONDON • NEW YORK

Morehouse Publishing
P.O. Box 13321
Harrisburg, PA 17105
Morehouse is a Continuum imprint.

Design by Corey Kent

Library of Congress Cataloging-in-Publication Data

Douglas, Deborah Smith.
The Praying Life: Seeking God in All Things / Deborah Smith Douglas.—
1st ed.
p. cm.
Includes bibliographical references.
ISBN 0-8192-1936-3 (pbk.)
1. Spiritual life. I. Title.
BV4501.3 .D68 2003
248.4—dc21
2002153483

Printed in the United States of America

03 04 05 06 07 08 6 5 4 3 2 1

To David

Contents

Acknowledgements

THIS BOOK WOULD NEVER have happened without the patience, generosity, and encouragement of a great many people. I am especially grateful to John Mogabgab of *Weavings,* who nurtured nearly half of these pieces into print in the first place, and who has been a gift from God in my writing life. My friends and fellow writers Nancy Arnon Agnew, Richard Holland, Annie Piper, and Cindy Quicksall Landsberg have been extraordinarily helpful and endlessly supportive readers of much of this material in draft form. To Mary Ann Holland, spiritual director par excellence, I am thankful for her "holy listening" to many of the experiences behind the words. Sister Mary Joaquin Bitler, S.C., has been a deep well of spiritual and literary encouragement for many years, as has Bishop Robert Morneau, valued reader and friend. Jane Gee, Ann Rowe, Becky Donohue, Christine Johnson, Bud Redding, Nan Schwandfelder, and Julie Smith—bless you for your steadfast friendship and support of my writing.

Thanks to Debra Farrington at Morehouse, who first proposed this book and who negotiated the initial rapids of publication with me, and to Nancy Fitzgerald, who saw the project into the light of ink at last.

I owe more than I can say to my husband David, on whose strength and wisdom and clarity I have relied, as wife and writer and fellow pilgrim, for more than a quarter century. Finally, thanks to our daughters Katie and Emily, whose now-vanished childhoods are present in these pages, in and between the lines.

Introduction

I CONFESS TO YOU, my brothers and sisters: I never did actually decide to lead a praying life, much less write a book about it. Unlike the infant Samuel, I was not consecrated at birth to the service of God. Unlike Therese of Lisieux's childhood, mine did not burn with the clear flame of an unmistakable religious vocation. Presbyterian girls growing up in Kansas in the 1950s, as I did, were not generally encouraged in that direction: Girl Scouts, yes; Carmelite convents, no.

But looking back, I can see that my life has been blessed, and full of God—as naturally, and as quietly, as the day is filled with light. Like C. S. Lewis, I have encountered "patches of Godlight in the woods of my experience."[1] Without my ever really intending it, my own life—as a wife and mother, daughter and friend—has taught me to see God hidden in the ordinary, to watch for God under the surface of things as a fisherman watches for fish.

Whether we recognize it or not, as C. S. Lewis noted, the world is "crowded" with God: "We may ignore, but we can nowhere evade, the presence of God, [who] walks everywhere *incognito,*" and whose disguise "is not always hard to penetrate. The real labor is to remember, to attend. In fact, to come awake."[2]

The essays and poems that make up this book reflect the ways I have come to remember and attend, to be awake to the presence of God. They are a record of the slow, cumulative gift of my own praying life, the ways I have learned to seek God in all things.

These ways could hardly be more prosaic: The small epiphanies of my life have come (as the pieces gathered here reflect) while I was standing in line at the post office, trying clumsily to start a fire in a woodstove, catching a bus, having breakfast with my five-year-old daughter, visiting an elderly woman in a nursing home, meeting a friend for lunch.

Of course, a praying life will not always be easy, or safe, or free from pain—no life is. There are, as the poet Virgil wrote, tears at the heart of things. But God is present even in those tears; God knows our suffering. Our inevitable times of grief or darkness can take us deeper into prayer, not only for our own healing but to enlarge our capacity for love. If we see the world with eyes that have wept, we may be ready to enter more deeply, with God, into the suffering of the broken world.

A praying life can be nearly any kind of life: married or celibate, public or "hidden," quiet or full of urgent demands. We need not quit our jobs or leave our families or strain anxiously after perfection. The invitation is simply to realize that "the only way to live," as the Trappist monk Thomas Merton understood, is in a world "charged with the presence and reality of God."[3]

This way of living is both deeply mysterious and blessedly ordinary. Embracing it, we will increasingly find ourselves finding God in all things. This is possible, by grace, because God is always seeking us, longing to be found. "Behold, I stand at the door and knock," Jesus tells us (Rev 3:20). God, like the father of the prodigal, runs to meet us while we are still on the way (see Luke 15:20).

We can—and with God's help, we will—come to see that the universe is incandescent with God's glory. "It will flame out, like shining from shook foil,"[4] the poet Gerard Manley Hopkins declared. The more we perceive this, the more we will be filled with awestruck joy. But the experience is given us not just for our delight and consolation; the delight is "heavy with responsibilities," as the French Jesuit Teilhard de Chardin observed.[5]

Living a praying life will make us instruments of God's peace, agents of God's love, propelling us to "work for mercy, order, beauty . . . to mend where we find things broken."[6] This is our vocation as Christians, our response to the call of God.

This response will be as various as we are numerous. No one's praying life, no one's journey into God, will look exactly like anyone else's. But it does seem to have a distinctive shape: a movement from awareness of God's presence to participation in God's love.

This formula—realization of God's presence, trust in God's purposes, deep availability to God's will—may strike us as arbitrary or artificial.[7] I believe, however, that it reflects a completely natural rhythm. I assimilated it entirely without meaning to, as a child, reading C. S. Lewis's Chronicles of Narnia.

When I was about ten years old, my father built a tree house for me, a sturdy platform in a huge old elm tree in our garden. It was complete with a little rope ladder I could pull up after me to ensure my privacy, and another rope with a basket tied to it to haul books up into my leafy solitude. I spent many peaceful hours there, reading everything I could find. Especially I read of Narnia, devouring the tales of Lucy and the other children discovering a way into Narnia through the wardrobe in the professor's house, of their vital role in rescuing Narnia from the evil tyranny of the White Witch, of their returns to Narnia in other perilous times. I was particularly drawn to Aslan, the great regal Lion, so full of power and love.

Throughout the children's adventures in the land of Narnia, the pattern is the same: Over and over again they find (or are found by) Aslan; they (especially Lucy) delight in his presence and respond to his will; increasingly they offer themselves to his saving purposes for Narnia.

There it was, the complete dynamic of the praying life, unconsciously but firmly under my skin, in my bones, before I was twelve. No wonder the lives of the saints, and the classic works on spiritual disciplines, when I came to read them as an adult, sounded oddly familiar, a distant echo of the horn of Aslan, "cool and sweet as music over water, but strong enough to shake the woods."[8]

Reading the Gospels also wakened echoes of that Narnian horn: I probably accepted (for example) the condensed account of Jesus healing Simon Peter's mother-in-law as authoritative because it had the same shape as Lucy's encounters with Aslan: Jesus "came and took her by the hand and lifted her up, and the fever left her; and she served them" (Mark 1:31). There it is again, in a single sentence, the outline of a praying life: presence, recognition, self-giving.

The story of blind Bartimaeus is another example of the spontaneous pattern of a praying life (see Mark 10:46-52). Even in his blindness, sitting at the side of the road that Jesus and the disciples and a great crowd were traveling, Bartimaeus knew Jesus was near and cried to him, "Jesus, Son of David, have mercy on me!" Jesus stopped and called Bartimaeus to come to him; the blind beggar threw off his cloak and "sprang up and came to Jesus." Jesus restored his sight, and Bartimaeus "followed him on the way."

The dynamic that characterizes the praying life is perhaps most intensely distilled in the Eucharist. We celebrate the real presence of Christ in the bread and wine and in the community gathered together; we declare our joy in that presence; we proclaim our reliance on its nourishing power by going to meet Christ at the altar. Then, thus strengthened, we are sent into the world "in peace, to love and serve the Lord." As I once heard a priest say at the close of the liturgy, "The Mass is ended; the world is waiting." Every day, all over the world, every time the bread is broken and the wine poured out, the Church enacts and embodies the essence of the praying life: presence, recognition, self-giving.

This pattern at the heart of the praying life has informed not only the substance but also the structure of this book.

The essays and poems that follow have been gathered loosely into sections; the first explores various kinds of prayer, ways of becoming more profoundly aware of God's presence in the world. The second section suggests that we can, knowing God to be near us, offer our weakness to God's strength in obedience and trust, as Bartimaeus did. The third section speaks of our becoming more fully members of the Body of Christ, as loving and serving God increasingly engages us in loving and serving others. Finally, the last section presents images of fruitfulness, ways of being faithful and present to the One who is unfailingly faithful and present to us, ready to do whatever God asks of us, even if that is something we—like the children in Narnia—would otherwise never have dreamed of doing, and something we know we could never do alone.

Robert Frost once said that a poem "begins in delight and ends in wisdom."[9] Our praying lives, it seems to me, begin in awareness and end in love. From any perception that God is real and present and active in the world, and any desire for a more profound experience of that presence, we will be led ever deeper into the boundless love God has for all creation.

I devoutly hope this small book will affirm and strengthen your own praying life as you seek God in all things.

Lord, teach us to seek you, and reveal yourself to us as we seek; for unless you instruct us we cannot seek you, and unless you reveal yourself we cannot find you. Let us seek you in desiring you; let us desire you in seeking you. Let us find you in loving you; let us love you in finding you.
—St. Anselm of Canterbury (1033–1109)

Part 1:
Ways of Praying

– 1 –

Be of Few Words

Her Majesty's War on Verbosity

THERE I WAS, standing in line at the post office again, my arms full of letters to send home to the United States from Scotland, when the handwritten notice caught my eye. Substantially reduced postal rates would be available for the holidays, the Royal Mail announced, for unsealed greeting cards containing no more than five words in addition to the printed message and the sender's name.

Five words? Five measly words? Heavens, why bother? I wondered to myself, rearranging the slippery stacks of thick (extra-postage-required) envelopes I was carrying. What on earth could one say that is worth saying in five words or less?

I beguiled my time in the queue by pondering this weighty question. "Merry Christmas—Happy New Year" would of course fit within the required brevity. But unless the cards' printed message was more than usually beside the point, this would surely be redundant, as well as being rather obvious, and unimaginative in the extreme. There was the urgently telegraphic and classically melodramatic "All discovered—flee at once," moderately unorthodox as Christmas greetings go but unarguably five words. The awkwardly banal "All well here; how there?" also briefly occurred to me, but on the whole I felt the five-word limit reflected a stinginess unbecoming the Royal Mail and dismissed the matter from my mind.

Then, unbidden, my memory produced the haunting final message of Etty Hillesum, scribbled on a scrip of paper and tossed from the window of a train bound for the death camps: "Tell them we left singing."

Five words. Five measly words. Containing whole worlds of sorrow, love, and courage.

So. Maybe it *was* possible to communicate meaningfully in five words or less. Christmas greetings aside, perhaps there were moments in human experience—and instances in the English language—where the *mot juste* was just five.

I posted my letters (paying a shocking penalty for the privilege of verbosity) and walked back across town, muttering to myself and counting on my fingers, intrigued as by a crossword puzzle by Her Britannic Majesty's pentagrammic challenge. I began rummaging in my rag-bag English-major mind for quotations, recalling Elizabeth Barrett Browning's parallel fives: "How do I love thee? Let me count the ways" (which would presumably have cost her double), and Emilia's anguished "Who hath done this deed?" from Othello III:5, and Desdemona's dying (and even more condensed) reply: "Nobody: I myself. Farewell."

I was hooked. All the rest of that day and well into the following week, I found myself weighing the treasures of the English language in postal scales. I counted (under my breath) the words of my favorite poems, of famous quotes, of conversations heard in the street.

Then I turned my search to Scripture and was overwhelmed by fives. I was astounded to discover, leafing though my Bible, how many of the passages I had marked over the years happened to consist of five words. Many of the most powerful promises in all of Holy Writ are wholly writ in fives. (In English translation at any rate; whether the original Hebrew and Greek are even more austerely economical, I do not, alas, know.)

God's word to Moses by the light of the burning bush, "I will be with you"; Jesus' triumphant "I have overcome the world"; and Mary Magdalene's ringing Easter witness "I have seen the Lord" all are cinquefoil, as it were.

So many of Jesus' words are familiar to us in clusters of five: "I am the good shepherd," "Your faith has healed you," "Rise and have no fear," "My peace I leave you." The Hebrew scriptures as well bloom with five-petaled flowers: "I know you by name," "I will send an angel," "Love is strong as death." Similarly, the vision of Saint John at Patmos—the insight that "death shall be no more"—manages to express one of our faith's essential convictions in five little words. And there is the divine economy of "light shines in the darkness" and "this Jesus God raised up." Perhaps my own personal favorite, one wonder of brevity set like a gem in another, is "Jesus said to her, 'Mary.'"

It is not only blessed assurance that comes in quinary, of course. Think of the serpent in Eden, beguiling Eve with "You will be like God." Or one of Abraham's least golden moments when, surrounded by lascivious Egyptians, he whispered to Sarah, "Say you are my sister."

Admonitions seem naturally to lend themselves to pentamerous compression: Scripture positively brims with five-leaved proverbs and aphorisms: "Go and sin no more," "Serve the Lord with gladness." Similarly, some of the poignant prayers in the Bible consist of five words: "Lord, have mercy on me," "Make haste to help me," "I believe; help my unbelief!" And Thomas, unforgettable, utterly unambiguous, "My Lord and my God."

Desolation as well seems to fit into quintupled phrases: the devastating "all the disciples forsook him" could be a Holy Week meditation all by itself, as of course could Jesus' cry from the cross, "Why hast thou forsaken me?" And for me, one of the most perfect visual brushstrokes in the Gospels is the detail from the story of the disciples on the Emmaus road: "They stood still, looking sad."

The more I browsed, the more I came up with handfuls of fives. Her Majesty's limitation, which at first had seemed so arbitrary and unreasonable—so ungenerous—began to appear almost recklessly extravagant. After all, so many powerful sayings are compacted into four words—Mother Julian's visionary "All shall be well," for instance. And how could Peter have borne another syllable in Jesus' piercing "Do you love me?"

Come to think of it, some deeply significant affirmations, invitations, promises, dramas, and blessings consist of three words: "So Abram went," "He is risen!" "Come and see," "Go in peace," "Jesus is Lord."

Or two! I recalled how moved I had been, on the remote Hebridean isle of Iona, by the inscription on the watchtower of the lonely abbey church: "Stand fast." What compressed sorrow lies in "Jesus wept," what immensities of self-offering are implied in "Yes, Lord."

For that matter, didn't one word often say what most needed to be said? Surely "Alleluia" and "Amen" are all we really need most of the time.

By the end of the week (much of which I had spent secretly counting the words of, and lamenting the excesses of, telephone conversations, newspaper headlines, and public service announcements on the radio), I was convinced that five words—or four, or three, or even two—can speak volumes. Just as a memorable meal can be prepared from a few simple ingredients, so can a feast of meaning be conveyed by an apparent dearth of words. There is a lesson for my loquacious spirit here, a deep learning about fasting and feasting, about self-discipline, about simplicity and silence.

Perhaps Emily Dickinson summed it up when she observed that "the banquet of abstemiousness effaces that of wine" (even if it did take her eight words to say it).

– 2 –

How I Pray Now

Sometimes, No Words at All

"HOW DO YOU PRAY NOW?" I like the question. It implies change; it implies that prayer—like any other profound, committed, intimate relationship—is dynamic. It will change, will grow and develop in response to changing circumstances. Like the Santa Fe River near where I live, our prayer sometimes overflows its banks, sometimes diminishes to the merest life-sustaining trickle, sometimes cuts a whole new course in the landscape.

The question "How do I pray now?" has been for me an invitation to get, as it were, an aerial view of the river—a chance to look back and see the riparian loops and bends, the shallow places and the rapids, the floodplains and the dams. It is all the same river—I can see that clearly from this airborne vantage point. The continuity, so often hidden in the small view of daily life, is revealed. And my river, while sometimes dallying in near-stagnation, sometimes choked by debris, sometimes even appearing to flow backward, continues stubbornly to seek the sea.

This continuity in my prayer life is perhaps most apparent in its external forms. Most mornings for over a decade, I have risen early for a quiet time before the crowded day begins; I participate in the community prayer of the Eucharist at least once a week; I am grateful for annual retreats; volunteer service to the larger community keeps me balanced and connected to the world; regular conversations with my spiritual director provide invaluable clarity and support.

All of these spiritual disciplines are important to me; none is optional. It is in the totality of them, woven together, that my life in God is sustained. Interior prayer without corporate worship tends toward self-preoccupation, and without guidance tends toward self-delusion; service without a faith context becomes "dead works." Nevertheless, daily private prayer is what I would like to look at now—partly because it is the anchor for so much else, and perhaps also because it is the part that has undergone the most change, and changed the most significantly, over the course of the years.

Thirty years ago I was in law school, where I systematically (painfully) trained my somewhat dreamy English-major mind to jump through hoops of adversarial argument and method. It has taken me a long time to recognize—much less to undo—the damage this hard-won way of thinking did to my praying. For many years I (unconsciously, of course) treated prayers as legal briefs, or at least as business letters. ("Holy and Ever Living God, Dear Sir:") Sometimes I prayed as though I were an attorney presenting a case before the divine judge, seeking by my eloquence, my logic, my sure grasp of the issues and keen sense of justice, to persuade the Heavenly Court to a certain course of action. Sometimes I prayed as though I were the firm's efficient executive secretary, bringing urgent lists and messages to the attention of the overworked senior partner who, without my help, could hardly be expected to establish priorities or even to recognize crises.

These days, by the grace of God, my prayer has changed. I pray these days with much less conviction of my own importance in (ever so tactfully) setting an agenda for God's busy day, and much more of an awestruck sense of the great privilege of simply participating in God's eternal love, letting it shine through my life as unobstructed as possible, like sunlight through clear glass. In other words, I seek now not so much to be the Supreme Court's star turn as—in the words of George Herbert—"to be a window, though God's grace."

Consequently, my prayers of intercession are much more trusting and quiet, much less insistently partisan and vocal than they once were. When I remember before God the pain of the world, I am less concerned with verbal eloquence than I used to be, much less implicitly sure that my job in prayer is somehow to change God's mind. In fact—except for the Collect for Purity at the beginning of my prayer time and the Lord's Prayer at the end—sometimes my prayers for others have no words at all, merely a sense of lifting those I love or ache for into God's infinitely compassionate hands.

It is not only the shape of my intercessory prayer that has changed with time, but also the way I pray with Scripture. As a

Protestant born and bred, I have always been deeply aware of the importance of the biblical revelation of God's purpose for human life. Bible study and Bible school were part of my life from the time I could read. By the time I was eight I could recite all the books of the Bible in order, from Genesis to Revelation; I had memorized several psalms in their entirety and could quote chapter and verse for most of the more memorable promises in Scripture. On my wedding day I carried a white leather-bound Bible, a gift from my mother, along with my bridal bouquet. When I began the practice of daily prayer, I brought not only the Bible into the morning quiet but also *Strong's Exhaustive Concordance* and *Peake's Commentary*—a well-intentioned but unwieldy lapful that pretty effectively ensured that my praying-with-Scripture would stay firmly in my head, far more intellectual and cognitive than meditative or receptive. I learned a great deal during this time in my life, but it was much ado about critical method and hermeneutics and had precious little to do with listening for the word of God in my own experience.

It has taken our patient God years to open my heart and quiet my endless earnest picking apart of Holy Writ. More than any other single factor in this transforming of my scriptural prayer, a graced experience of Ignatian spirituality helped me to glimpse the possibilities of praying with the imagination and heart as well as with the intellect.

Several years ago, I made an individually guided eight-day retreat at a Jesuit retreat house, where for the first time I encountered the distinctively Ignatian way of praying with Scripture. The retreat began with an initial conference with my assigned director, who gave me a biblical text, and suggestions for a way of praying with it that involved my imagination and memory as well as my mind. Each day thereafter, I met with my director for an hour, to confide the content and quality of my prayer, and to receive another passage for meditation. Aside from these meetings and daily Mass in the chapel, the rest of each day was spent alone and in silence. That was a week of special blessing; the depth and power of the meditations took my breath away. As a Christ-centered, biblically grounded Protestant, with years of the gentle discipline of *lectio divina* behind me, I thought I knew—thought I had always known—what it means to "pray with Scripture," but I was wrong. Unconsciously but inevitably, I was limiting the operation of divine grace to the Calvinist dictum of *sola scriptura*, clinging stubbornly to the written word in a way that kept the Living Word from entering my heart. Under the wise guidance of my Jesuit director, in the blessed quiet of the place, by the grace of God, I was led that week to a whole new understanding of "real presence" in scriptural prayer—a radically sacramental sense of actual encounter with Christ, who is "in, with, and under" the narrative.

Needless to say, that retreat has profoundly influenced "how I pray now." When I compose myself to reflect, in the presence of God, on a passage in Scripture, I am no longer seeking the definitive scholarly interpretation of the text. Instead, I am offering my whole self—imagination, memory, intellect, desire—to the whispered Word of God. I am open to divine surprises; I let the river go where it will.

These, then, are two specific ways in which the way I pray now has deeply changed from the way I used to pray: When I intercede for others, I am more offering myself to be an instrument of God's peace than I am lobbying for a particular result; when I pray with Scripture I am offering myself to the Living Word rather than clinging to the written word. "Offer" seems to be the operative verb here—more and more, my prayer is more listening than talking, more giving than asking.

Consequently—back to the river again—the way I pray is increasingly "without ceasing," as silent, steady, and active as a river flowing through the land.

The African-American poet Langston Hughes spoke of this transforming dynamic at the very heart of who we are:

I've known rivers ancient as the world
and older than the flow of human blood in human veins.
My soul has grown deep like the rivers.

I would like to think that my soul has—once and for all—"grown deep like the rivers," that my prayer, my whole life in God, has reached a place of permanent quiet depth and power beyond change. I know it is not so: It is not in the nature of rivers not to change, and I am sure God is not finished with me yet. But I do hope that God will give me the grace not to struggle against the changes too much, not to rush in—self-willed as the Army Corps of Engineers—to build dams or embark on diversion schemes. I hope I can stay open to the Spirit of God in my listening and always trust in the limitless and everlasting sea toward which, however slowly, I still wind my way.

I love Ezekiel's vision of the sacred river that flows from the throne of God, deep and mighty, "a river that I could not pass through, for the water had risen; it was deep enough to swim in." Wherever the river goes, it gives life: "When it enters the stagnant waters of the sea, the water will become fresh. . . . Everything will live where the river goes" (Ezek 47:5, 8-9). I thank God for the river that runs through all of life, for waters that baptize us ever deeper into the new creation, for prayer that is alive and "deep enough to swim in."

— 3 —

New Wine

Praying the Scriptures

AT THE HEART OF Ignatian spirituality is the experience of "praying the Scriptures"—a way of prayer that unites thinking and feeling, remembering and imagining. For me, one of the most amazing graces of this form of prayer is the way even the most familiar biblical texts often take on a whole new life, revealing depths of meaning and presence that even the most scholarly "bible study" can be powerless, by itself, to uncover.

Rather than elaborate the method, I have chosen to share the experience. I hope this set of meditations on the story of the wedding at Cana—prayerfully imagined in the voices of four people present and transformed by Jesus' presence there—will amount to an invitation to pray with and in the Scriptures with a new freedom. God grant, in all our engagement with Scripture, that having the eyes of our hearts enlightened, we may know the hope to which Christ has called us (Eph 1:18).

> On the third day there was a wedding in Cana of Galilee, and the mother of Jesus was there. Jesus and his disciples had also been invited to the wedding. When the wine gave out, the mother of Jesus said to him, "They have no wine." And Jesus said to her, "Woman, what concern is that to you and to me? My hour has not yet come." His mother said to the servants, "Do whatever he tells you." Now standing there were six stone water jars for the Jewish rites of purification, each holding twenty or thirty gallons. Jesus said to them, "Fill the jars with water." And they filled them up to the brim. He said to them, "Now draw some out, and take it to the chief steward." So

they took it. When the steward tasted the water that had become wine, and did not know where it came from (though the servants who had drawn the water knew), the steward called the bridegroom and said to him, "Everyone serves the good wine first, and then the inferior wine after the guests have become drunk. But you have kept the good wine until now." Jesus did this, the first of his signs, in Cana of Galilee, and revealed his glory; and his disciples believed in him. (John 2:1-11 NRSV

The Maidservant Remembers

It was all so quiet. Nobody knew, then, what had happened, except for his mother and us servants. I am not even sure myself just what happened, even now. Much less how. He never touched the water. He never touched the jars, or the cup I filled at his command. He didn't even say anything special. There was that brief exchange between the two of them, mother and son, and then a sort of stillness in the midst of the noise of the party. (Thank goodness nobody realized we had run out of wine.)

All I know is, I did what he told me. Miriam and I carried water from the well to fill the big stone jars, empty now after the ritual cleansing before the meal. We filled them to the top. I remember how the water swelled and trembled at the brim but did not spill. It was perfectly ordinary water, I swear; I carried it myself, and poured it in. I didn't even know what he meant to do; I just did what he told me.

And when he told me to, I drew it out again, a cupful to take to the steward of the feast. Only then, it wasn't water anymore. It was wine. The water was now wine. I nearly dropped the cup when I saw it. I didn't say anything, but Miriam and I stared at each other and then turned to stare at him.

His eyes met ours steadily, and there was laughter in them, and a kind of exhilaration, and a kind of resignation too. Almost as though more than the water had been changed. As though something even bigger than that had happened. As though something was beginning, really—for him, and for us all.

I know it sounds strange, but I couldn't help feeling, holding that cup of new wine that had never been grapes, that somehow everything had changed, forever. Something had started that could not be stopped, and nothing would ever be the same.

All I know is, I did what he told me. And you know what? I think the water did too.

The Bride Remembers

I was miserable when the wine gave out. Not so much embarrassed, even though it was my own wedding and I suppose any bride would be humiliated to begin her married life that way. But it was worse than that. It seemed an omen, and a bleak one, for my whole life.

I knew that Jacob was not happy about the marriage our fathers had arranged. I have always known he would have preferred my younger sister—she is prettier and livelier than I. Even at the wedding feast he couldn't help watching her as she laughed and danced with the other young girls. But I hadn't known he was so displeased as this—so reluctant as to fail to provide enough wine for our guests to drink our health and happiness.

What kind of life could I expect with such a man? I sat in silence, staring into my empty cup, trying not to think of years stretching out ahead as empty, as joyless, as that.

But then I heard a burst of laughter from the steward and saw him bearing a jug through the crowd to my husband's place at the table. He splashed some wine into a cup and raised it exuberantly, saying something about saving the good wine until now. I think Jacob was as startled as I was—we had both known, separated by the length of the table though we were, that there was no wine left. Wearily I had thought, At least we share the knowledge of what we lack.

But here was wine. Out of nowhere, out of nothing. Jacob sent a pitcherful down to my end of the table, and he met my eyes as he raised his cup to me in a silent salutation. Gratitude and astonishment and relief flashed between us and drew us for a moment close together.

Who knows where it came from? I drank deep, and gladly. Some unexpected gift, I supposed, and thanked God for it, and for the unknown guest who had provided it.

There were many things I did not know or understand, I reflected as I felt the wine warm my cold flesh, and hope spread like fire in my veins. Perhaps the future was not as empty as I had thought. Perhaps this marriage held not so meager a prospect. If this could happen, anything could.

Perhaps my full cup was an omen more powerful than the empty one had been. God grant it so. God grant us long life together, and many surprises to encounter, together, along the way.

I raised my cup to my new husband and—for the first time—smiled at him from my heart.

A Guest Remembers

It certainly wasn't much of a wedding. Just an ordinary provincial do. I would so much rather not have come at all. Our youngest son was ill of a fever at home in Capernaum; I didn't know anyone in Cana—and Jewish celebrations are so tribal. I always feel awkward and out of place. Unwelcome, really, although I suppose people are polite enough.

But Julius takes his official responsibilities seriously and was pleased that we had been invited. Tensions with Rome have been getting worse lately in Galilee, and he felt it was important that we both attend. So there I was. Smiling fixedly at strangers, wishing I were at home, wishing I had worn a different gown, wishing I had another glass of wine.

I heard a whisper pass through the crowd like a breeze, a rumor that there was no more wine. Catastrophe. Even in the provinces. But it can't have been true, because in fact suddenly there were rivers of wine, oceans of wine at that village wedding. I have never seen such abundance, even in Rome, and it wasn't that raw Galilean stuff we've gotten used to. In fact, it was marvelous. The best wine I have ever tasted.

I must have raised my eyebrows in astonishment over the rim of my cup, because suddenly Julius was grinning at me wryly. I remembered my manners, and my duty, and turned with well-practiced graciousness to speak to the inconspicuous woman seated next to me. Some relative of the bride, I think she was, an aunt or something. But I forgot my dignity and Julius's position—I forgot even my aching head and anxious heart, because I was so struck by the woman's face.

The face of a woman no longer young, it was both serene and

deeply marked by sorrow. Very much a mother's face. But what arrested my commonplace remark was the clear impression of something enormous happening to her at that very moment.

She looked as though she had just been given a princely gift, or had just given something priceless away. Or as if she had just heard some long-awaited news—or as though she were listening for something, the way all mothers do. Almost as though—absurd thought—she were the mother of all living.

An odd impression. I tried to shake it off, attributing the unaccustomed fancy to the really extraordinary wine. I ended up not speaking to her at all—oddly enough, it would have felt presumptuous—but the wordless smile she gave me lit up the whole room.

That evening ended better than it began. That evening, in fact, felt like the beginning of something important. I have never forgotten that woman's face or the excellence of that wine. For some reason I date our real life in Galilee (as opposed to our exile here) from that night. It was the first time we felt welcome in a Jewish home, invited to a party that seemed suddenly, for a moment, to include the whole world.

Nathanael Remembers

I never thought it would begin like that. Of course, I had scarcely had time to think at all. It had only been the day before that the whole thing had started, when Philip hauled me over to meet him. It was his knowing about that business under the fig tree that made me realize who he must be. Knowing who he was, I would have followed him anywhere, even to the ends of the earth. I knew the others felt the same. We were ready for anything.

But the very first thing we did, the very next day, was follow him to a hometown wedding. It didn't seem awfully auspicious, really—not even much of a party. I've known those two kids all my life, of course, and naturally I wish them well, but it wasn't exactly festive, as wedding feasts go. They even ran out of wine.

And that is when it happened. I don't think anybody else saw it, except for his mother—it was her idea—and a couple of the servants, but Peter and I were leaning against the wall next to the water jars, nursing the last of the sour local wine that was all poor Jacob had come up with.

We saw it, all right. We saw the servants fill the jars with water;

we saw them take out wine. But if we hadn't seen it, we never would have known where it came from.

I felt Peter stiffen beside me. They were drawing the wine out by the pitcherful now, and someone splashed a bit on his tunic, where a stain spread dark as blood. "So much, Lord?" I heard him whisper, and for a second—I was pretty flabbergasted, you understand, and not quite thinking straight—I thought he was talking about blood, not wine. But there was much wine indeed—all six jars, each up to my shoulder, filled to the brim with the best wine Cana has ever tasted, before or since. It was far more than enough—Judas always shook his head disapprovingly when he heard the story afterward—and far better than it needed to be.

A strange way for the whole thing to begin. Water and wine and small-town weddings and low-key miracles were not our idea, in those days, of the way to establish a kingdom. But it was the beginning, and it was enough.

Just for a second there, just as he had promised—right there among the wedding guests and the wine cups and the water jars—I had a glimpse of heaven opened, a glimpse of angels going up and down.

And so it began.

— 4 —

To See with the Eyes of the Heart

IN GEORGE BERNARD SHAW'S PLAY *Saint Joan*, Captain Robert (described in the stage notes as a "self-assertive, loud-mouthed" military squire) is interrogating the young Joan of Arc. He is particularly disdainful about the voices she claims to hear, the voices of St. Catherine and St. Margaret, who instruct her, in the name of God, to raise the siege of Orleans. Contemptuously, Captain Robert dismisses the possibility that these voices come from God—on the contrary, he insists, "they come from your imagination."

Joan replies, "Of course. That is how the messages of God come to us."[1]

Joan, in the simplicity and clarity of those close to God, stakes her life on the dangerous possibility that God may speak through our imaginations. She knows that what we imagine can be real, and precious, and sacred. Unfortunately, what saints (and poets, and children) may take serenely for granted is not always so clear to the rest of us.

Imagination is a quality that tends to be denigrated by sensible folk, who insist on what is tangible and rational and seem to equate the imaginative with the mad, the frivolous, or the deluded. In the Church, a deep distrust of "graven images" and a preference for "right thinking" can starve our minds and hearts of much of the richness of Scripture, poetry, and our own experience. We can, like Captain Robert, refuse to believe that God can speak to us through our imaginations. Especially those of us who come, as I do, from iconoclastic Calvinist stock may be suspicious of the religious imagination. We may even resist "the messages of God" unless they conform to our prosaic norms of plausibility and rationality.

Fortunately, God is wonderfully inventive and patient with us, finding all sorts of creative ways to "steal past the watchful dragons"[2] that jealously guard our minds. Memories, dreams, intuition, prayer "too deep for words"—these gifts from God operate within us at a level far beyond conscious control or intellectual understanding. They function, in fact, through our imaginations, rather than our intellect. Interestingly, St. Thomas Aquinas declared that that is how angels influence us—not through our intellect or will, but through our senses and imagination.[3]

Wim Wenders is a German filmmaker who has a marvelous instinctive sense of this truth. His film *Wings of Desire* is a speculative flight of thoughtful fancy about angels among us. In an interview, Wenders pondered the way angels seek to influence us, and suggested that "the angel realizes that the goal is not to talk into your ears, but to try and live in your eyes."[4] Not to impart information, but to change the way we see.

Angels at home in our eyes. How might we be changed if we saw the world through angels' eyes? Might it transform our vision, lead our lives into more harmony with the mind of Christ, help us to imagine what God has in store for us? Perhaps this is what St. Paul meant in his letter to the Ephesians when he speaks of his longing for the community there to have "the eyes of your hearts enlightened, that you may know what is the hope to which [Christ] has called you" (1:18).

The angels' longing for us to see a God-filled world—Paul's desire for us to see the hope of Christ with "the eyes of our hearts enlightened"—all seem to involve the right use and nurture of the imagination—not to delude ourselves about reality, but to open ourselves more fully to it. How can we possibly be people of faith unless we are people of imagination? How else can we allow ourselves to believe that Providence intends and includes more than we can see from the surface of our broken lives? Faith, as the writer of the letter to the Hebrews reminds us, "is the assurance of things hoped for, the conviction of things not seen" (11:1). It is only with "enlightened eyes"—with hearts open and committed to possibilities "not seen"—that we can lean into the kingdom.

The hope to which God has called us will certainly be more than we can imagine, but it will hardly be less. Trusting that God is beyond our ability to know as an intellectual/theological concept can open the eyes of our hearts to see the creative and transforming activity of God within and among us. Being attentive to memory, dream, and symbol can reveal God hidden in our midst. Like anything else in the spiritual life, this new way of seeing will involve us in both discipline and grace. Sometimes we need to learn to be more attentive, to listen to what God may be trying to tell us; sometimes all we have to do is get out of the way.

My childhood was, thanks be to God, unselfconsciously filled with companions from the worlds of fairy tale and myth. Without my realizing it, my solitary tree house hours with the talking beasts and valiant children of all seven volumes of C. S. Lewis's Narnia Chronicles, were, in C. S. Lewis's own phrase, "baptizing my imagination"—coming to live in my eyes, drawing my heart deeper into the strange possibilities of transformation at the heart of the gospel.

This great unrecognized gift surfaced in my adult life in an unexpected way. Late one night during my sophomore year at Duke University, I was standing alone by the bus stop on the main quadrangle. The library was closed, and I was waiting for the last bus that would take me back to my dorm. I was feeling particularly bleak at that moment in my life—lonely, frightened, sad. The old certainties of childhood were rocking beneath me, and grown-up life did not appear to have much to recommend it. Standing there, I noticed by the light of the street lamp that someone had painted huge pawprints—those of an enormous cat, it seemed—on the flagstone. Following them down the walkway, I saw that whoever it was had painted "Aslan lives!" at the end of the path, where the pawprints stopped. The effect of this message was instantaneous and powerful. I knew, with a rush of tears to my eyes and of joy to my heart, that it was, simply, true.

I hadn't thought of Aslan in years, though he—the great Christlike lion in C. S. Lewis's Narnia Chronicles—had made himself at home in my imagination more than a decade before. I was not reflecting on allegory or metaphor; I did not analyze my reaction. I simply, with all my heart, recognized the transforming truth of the affirmation. Aslan is alive. Resurrection happens. Christ is risen. In a single leap, Aslan had bounded past the watchful dragons of my mind and all the intervening years to return—where he has remained—deep within my consciousness of God. Because my whole childhood rose up to greet the Lion, my tenuously sophisticated young-adult self had no defenses against the saving "Alleluia!" truth of that moment.

In his preface to *George MacDonald: An Anthology*, C. S. Lewis gratefully acknowledges his enormous debt to MacDonald for "baptizing his imagination":

> It must be more than thirty years ago that I bought—almost unwillingly, for I had looked at the volume on that bookstall and rejected it on a dozen previous occasions—the Everyman edition of *Phantases*. A few hours later I knew that I had crossed a great frontier. . . . What it actually did to me was to convert, even to baptize . . . my imagination. It did nothing to my intellect nor (at that time) to my conscience. Their turn came far later and with the help of many other books and men. But when the process was complete—by which, of course, I mean "when it had really begun"—I found that I was still with MacDonald and that he had accompanied me all the way. . . . The quality which had enchanted me in his imaginative works turned out to be the quality of the real universe, the divine, magical, terrifying and ecstatic reality in which we all live."[5]

The debt Lewis owed to MacDonald is one I dearly owe to him: Without Aslan and Puddleglum and Lucy and Prince Caspian under my imaginative belt, I might never have recognized the claiming reality of Christ Risen at that bus stop.

Such sacramental moments of encounter and transformation are, of course, pure gift—"prevenient grace," one of the ways God comes running to meet us while we are still on the way (or even standing still, waiting for a bus). These moments—part memory, part intuition, part imagination, part prayer—can happen to us at any time.

It helps, of course, to have been since childhood a "friend of Narnia"—but it is certainly not necessary. Even if, like Eustace Clarence Scrubbs in the third volume of Narnia, we have "read only the wrong books, [those with] a lot to say about exports and imports and governments and drains,"[6] we may come—also like Eustace—joyfully to know and be known by the Lion, to have our hearts enlightened and our whole way of seeing radically changed.

If we begin to trust that God may be longing to meet us in all kinds of ways we can neither anticipate nor control, we can also learn to recognize these gift-moments when they occur. "Earth's crammed with heaven," Elizabeth Barrett Browning assures us, "and every common bush afire with God."[7] All we have to do is open the eyes of our heart and see it, hidden in plain sight.[8] Like birdwatchers, if we are willing to sit quietly and watch patiently, we may be in for some glorious surprises.

Years ago, when our daughters were very young, my husband, David, and I took them one February weekend to Bosque del Apache, a wild bird sanctuary in southern New Mexico where sandhill cranes and whooping cranes and snow geese spend the winter.

We had not realized just how cold and dark those marshes could be at five o'clock on a winter morning. We routed the girls out of bed in our motel in what felt like the middle of the night and took them, bundled in parkas and blankets, to stand in the freezing dark to await the dawn and the awakening of the birds. The girls were bewildered and less than half-awake. The geese, more sensible than we, were sound asleep, heads under wings, motionless and barely visible in the dark and mist of the marshes. Predawn, precoffee, the marrow freezing in my bones, my wintry imagination dwelt on sleep and death. We huddled beside the car in the dark and the cold, shifting around to try to keep warm, watching eerie wisps of mist rise from the ice-edged water, as the leaden sky lightened by almost imperceptible degrees.

And then it happened. The sun rose. Just as it appeared over the horizon, a silent flame of light and life, all the geese took flight at once. We instinctively ducked and laughed for startled joy—thousands of dormant creatures in a flash uprushing in unison. On the wing. On the wind. *En masse*. The sound was amazing—the whoosh of mighty wings, the honking call of mighty voices—but it was the sight that raised the hair on my neck. In that first instant of the new day, they took to the sky, the rising sun gilding ten thousand snowy wings. A vision of angels could hardly have been more stunning.

In that moment, I believe, I had an experience of the mystery of resurrection. A glimpse of what it might be like—something that sudden, that overwhelming, that glorious. The analogy was unbidden, spontaneous—pure gift. A flash of Easter mystery on a dreary Lenten morning. (The wild geese are flying; Aslan lives.)

Our word "religion" comes from the Latin root "religare," which means to bind, to connect. In some ways, our whole religious life can be seen as a process of making (and being made by) that kind of connection. Because I had loved Aslan as a child, I was open to the power of the resurrection through that hidden treasure of memory and imagination—open in a way, at a depth, not available to the more familiar credal statements of the same truth. Because that connection had taken root in me, and because by grace I had Easter growing somewhere at the center of who I was, I could, years later, rejoice with all my heart in the Paschal mystery present to my senses and imagination in a winter dawn full of wild geese flying. Webster's dictionary defines mystery as a religious truth revealed by God that humans cannot know by reason alone and that, once it has been revealed, cannot be completely understood. Experienced, yes—revealed and recognized, certainly—but not ultimately reduced to doctrinal prose.

This whole business of the "baptized imagination" is not just for saints and poets—it is for all of us. Joan herself, in Shaw's play, is quite clear on this point. Charles, King of France, is annoyed that God seems to speak to this peasant girl but not to him. "Oh, your voices, your voices. Why don't the voices come to me? I am king, not you." Again, Joan is swift to answer: "They do come to you; but you do not hear them. You have not sat in the field listening for them. When the angelus rings you cross yourself and have done with it; but if you prayed from your heart, and listened to the thrilling of the bells in the air after they stop ringing, you would hear the voices as well as I do."[9]

If we pray from our hearts, if we listen for the sound that bells make after they stop ringing, God will find a way past the watchful dragons; angels may come to live in our eyes. The eyes of our hearts will be enlightened. By grace we can come to stake our lives on what we can experience but never fully understand: the transforming reality of the saving love of God, "the divine, magical, terrifying and ecstatic reality in which we all live."[10]

Can you imagine?

– 5 –

Becoming Like Children

EVERY ONCE IN A WHILE I REALIZE—like Pooh Bear going downstairs: bumpedty-bump—what a lot I have to learn. Usually I realize at the same time what a great sense of humor God must have—and how true it is that those who live in Christ will have their world turned upside down.

All this simultaneous realizing is pretty tiring, of course, and also a bit discouraging sometimes. I am a grown-up now, after all, with the Seriously Grown-Up Responsibility of being both a mother and teacher, and I would like a little respect, please, and a bit of peace and quiet if you don't mind. Stability appeals to me, rather a lot.

As a cradle Presbyterian, I have spent most of my life in a tradition that places a premium on decency and order in the Christian life. As a busy wife and mother, I have a real stake in keeping—and encouraging my family to keep—domestic affairs well-organized and running smoothly. As a lawyer, I learned the value of predictability and control. As a teacher, I am quick to seize opportunities to instruct.

In other words, I spend a lot of time trying to hold the world right side up.

Therefore (God knows), I have a special need to be reminded that Jesus came to turn the world upside down, and that that has been, from the beginning, the mission of the Church (see Acts 17:6). I need to learn—again and again, it seems—that to be educated means to be led out, that to be faithful means to be open to surprises, that God may value joy and wonder as much as decency and order.

On two different occasions recently, young children have been instruments of grace to me, reversing my death-dealing sense of the fitness of things and inviting me into a new way of seeing God.

The first occurred when my five-year-old daughter asked me at breakfast one morning about her bedtime prayers. She wasn't really sure, she admitted, just what to say to God. (Now this is the sort of opening I like: "Mom, teach us to pray.") I poured orange juice and congratulated myself on such a splendid opportunity for age-appropriate instruction in confession and petition. "God likes to hear from us," I told Emily, "the same things all mommies and daddies like to hear from their children: please and thank you and I'm sorry."

Emily considered this, licking jam from her fingers in order to count to three: please; thank you; I'm sorry. She nodded, then waved the two unaccounted-for fingers and said, "Maybe there are two other things I say a lot that God would like to hear from me."

"What's that, honey?" I asked absently, beginning to clear the table (the lesson being over). "Maybe," she suggested, "I could tell God 'Wow!' and 'I love you.'"

I sat down, my hands full of silverware. Bumpedty-bump. "Yes, of course, darling, what a wonderful idea. Those are excellent prayers," I assured her, and sent her off to brush her teeth. But when I got up a few moments later, I was under no illusions about who had received the lesson. I had forgotten—as I so often forget—that prayer begins in praise and adoration. God had pulled my Grown-Up-In-Charge-of-Religious-Education authority right out from under me (with love and laughter, I am sure) as a means of reminding me.

It is, alas, all too easy to forget the centrality of adoration and delight in our worship, especially when we place priority on our own dignity before God in church.

As my own daughter innocently showed me how narrow and formal my personal prayer was in danger of becoming, it took another couple of children to reveal the peril of joylessness in my participation in corporate worship.

It has long been my custom to attend midweek Eucharist at an Episcopal church near us (supplementing my Sunday Presbyterianism with a Wednesday dose of liturgy and sacrament). The quiet of the service and the intimacy of the small gathering mean a great deal to me. So I was frankly annoyed one morning recently to see that our familiar (predominately elderly, decidedly staid) ranks had been swelled by a young couple new to the parish, accompanied by their little boy and baby girl. "Oh great," I grumbled to myself. "Suffer the little children to disrupt the service." (There are moments, I confess, when I sympathize with the harried disciples who wanted to send the children away, lest they bother the Busy and Important Grown-Ups in Charge.)

These children were sweet-natured and well-behaved; nevertheless, by the grace of God, they did indeed disrupt the service; they did indeed turn our decently-and-in-order expectations upside down.

When the dozen or so of the faithful present that morning gathered around the altar to receive Holy Communion, the priest blessed the babe in arms, making the sign of the cross on her infant forehead. For some reason this so charmed the baby that she laughed out loud, raising her flower of a face for more.

There isn't a more infectious sound under heaven than that of happy baby laughter, and every one of us immediately responded in kind, startled into shared delight. The baby beamed at all of us, and for once we received the Body and Blood with smiling joy instead of funereal gravity.

The baby's older brother was a poised five or six (participating in Communion as a baptized member of the parish, as is permitted in the Episcopal Church). He received the host, with his mother's help, and the priest lifted the chalice to his lips. Perhaps he had never received in both kinds before; perhaps he took rather a larger sip than he intended; perhaps it was his first taste of real wine. In any event, when the priest withdrew the chalice which had momentarily eclipsed his small face, the child's round eyes and dropped jaw expressed such thunderstruck astonishment that all of us adults very nearly laughed out loud again, and bit our lips instead, not lest the proprieties be violated but lest we embarrass the child. Bumpedty-bump. Another learning.

William Johnston, a Jesuit who lived for many years in Japan, tells the story somewhere of a conversation he once had with a Buddhist monk who was curious about Catholic ritual. "What happens in the Mass?" the monk wanted to know. Father Johnston explained the liturgy step by step. The monk listened carefully without interrupting for some time. "Then," Father Johnston continued, "the faithful come forward and receive the Body of Christ, and then go back to the pews and sing a song." "They what?" The Buddhist was incredulous. "They receive the Body of Christ—they take God into their mouths—and they can stand up? They can walk? They can sing?"

Christians receiving Communion, the Buddhist clearly felt, should be "astonished with a great astonishment, overcome with amazement," like the people who witnessed Jesus' raising of the little girl from the dead (see Mark 5:42), or like the little boy astounded by a taste of new wine.

Jesus blessing the children is, of course, a (perhaps dangerously) familiar image in our churches. Stained glass windows memorialize the text from Luke 18:16: "Let the children come to me, and do not hinder them." Sunday School posters glorify the "humbleness of this child" praised in Matthew 18:4.

There is a subtle danger here of distorting the Gospel's message. We do not well serve either children or the kingdom by sentimentalizing childhood into something it is not, nor by assuring ourselves that, unlike those awful disciples, we certainly do not forbid the children to approach Jesus. (On the contrary! Heavens, just look at the program designs, the staffing patterns! The curriculum options, the budget allocations!)

But there is another, sharper, point to the story. The people who were bringing the children to Jesus were doing so not that they might be biblically literate or politically correct. "They were bringing children to him," Mark's Gospel states clearly, "that he might touch them" (Mark 10:13-16).

Wise parents, those.

Jesus responded to the children by taking them in his arms and blessing them, laying his hands on them. He responded to the disciples with a warning: "Whoever does not receive the kingdom of God like a child shall not enter it" (Mark 10:15).

I wonder, reading Mark's Gospel and reflecting on these (blessed) children in my life, if the kind of childlike reception of the kingdom Jesus meant does not so much depend on photogenic innocence or gratifying humility as on wholehearted trust, spontaneous joy, and a willingness to risk surprises.

Perhaps after all, to be children of God, children of light, is—more than I ever dreamed—about being willing to have the world turned upside down.

To be flabbergasted, utterly amazed, at a taste of Communion wine. To be delighted into laughter at the touch of a blessing hand. To pray "Wow!" and "I love you" with the simplicity of a five-year-old. Could these be glimpses of what it might mean to "receive the kingdom of God like a child"? (Luke 18:17).

If so, then the image of children in the arms of Jesus is far more than a sentimental and possibly self-congratulatory reminder that children as well as adults are fully members of the family of faith. That image is also a warning to us that unless we "become like children, [we] will never enter the kingdom of heaven" (Matt 18:3).

There is an old story of St. Francis of Assisi that is also an image of the kingdom of God, the communion of saints: an apparently endless line of the faithful through the ages, trying to follow Jesus. They are careful, devout, intent on getting it right. Eyes on the ground, ignoring all else, fitting their feet as precisely as possible into the footsteps of the Master. At the very end of the procession follows Francis, paying no attention to his feet or to himself at all, but focused wholly on the One at the head of the line—dancing in joyful adoration, his feet falling spontaneously just where they need to be, just as Christ had led the way.

My daughter would understand that—discipleship as dancing. She would live that way, pray that way, if I "hindered her not."

Maybe even I could learn to live and pray like that, if I surrendered my need to get it right, my need (that I project on God) for all to be done decently and in order. If I could laugh for sheer delight at a blessing, if I could be overcome with amazement in the receiving of Communion, maybe by the grace of God even I might find myself saying yes to the kingdom of heaven.

Wow.

– 6 –

The Examen Reexamined

When I first learned in my Protestant childhood how to pray a kind of "examination of conscience," it was a frightening and discouraging experience—a sort of inept, private confession of sin without guidance and without absolution. "Remember your day," my Bible school teachers urged us, "and all the unkind and naughty things you did and said, and ask God to forgive you for them, and promise to try to be better tomorrow." A harmless practice, one would think, and a valuable one in theory: Those good women were attempting to instill in our heedless young hearts the beginnings of compunction and remorse, to hold out for us the ever-renewed possibility of God's patient mercy.

However, the only other bedtime prayer we knew inevitably informed the whole idea of conscience smitten at bedtime: "Now I lay me down to sleep. I pray Thee, Lord, my soul to keep. If I should die before I wake, I pray Thee, Lord, my soul to take." The terrible possibility of "if I should die before I wake" lurked darkly behind the urgent need to have sought and found all the day's sins before "I lay me down to sleep."

So, dutifully and anxiously, I would rummage through the day's events as I would have through a toy chest—but I was training myself to see only the broken toys. I searched diligently through heaps of beloved treasure, blind to everything that was not dented or torn or incomplete. It did not occur to me that God might delight, as I did, in the wholeness of what miraculously remained unspoiled; it certainly never crossed my mind that God might like to be present in my play. I never questioned God's odd preference for my worst, most fretful, selfish moments; naturally I had no idea how deeply I was shaping my image of God or my sense of myself.

So when, many years later, I was making my first individually guided Ignatian retreat[1] and my director suggested that I "pray the Examen" I thought (with a sinking heart) that I knew just what to do. But by the grace of God, I was wrong.

I discovered that week a whole new way of offering my life to God, one day at a time—a whole new and redemptive way of finding God present in all things. Gradually, I learned to invite God to be with me in the remembering itself: Together we sorted through the day's nets. While I still grieved, as I had as a child, over the precious things I had carelessly or willfully broken, I could also rejoice in discovering gifts received but perhaps not acknowledged—or even noticed—in the busyness of the moment. Most importantly, I was beginning to notice patterns and directions; I was beginning to move from self-scrutiny to discernment.

I learned, in short, that an examination of *conscience*—a single-minded, grim-hearted quest for sins—is not at all the same enterprise as an examination of *consciousness*, in which we look back over the day in order to find where God has been in it.[2]

After my retreat, in my growing appreciation for the Examen[3] as a particularly rich and fruitful form of prayer, I sought to learn more about it. One of the first things one sees, on examining the Examen, is that the purpose is not, as I had vaguely assumed in my childhood, the mere nightly emptying of the day's trash, lest we die "in our sins" before morning. Neither is the Examen primarily concerned with what good or bad actions we have done during the day—not that that lets us off the hook in any way. The broader way of praying is not at all a more shallow way. It is not a bit easier or "nicer"—a sort of watered-down confession of sin with the sting of self-knowledge taken out. Indeed, it is far deeper and more costly, more conducive to profound self-offering and interior transformation than the mere dispirited raking over of refuse that was my childish idea of "examining conscience."

On the contrary, the deep purpose—and effect—of the Examen is to change our way of seeing. The German film director Wim Wenders believes that that is how angels communicate the love of God to humans: "The angel realizes that the goal is not to talk into your ears, but to try and live in your eyes."[4]

If we pray the Examen regularly, generously, and courageously,

God will come and live in our eyes. Gradually, we will begin to see ourselves, and understand our actions, in a whole new way. Eventually, by the grace of God, we will begin to recognize God in all things, to rejoice in the invitational, relational love of God "unto whom all hearts are open, all desires known, and from whom no secrets are hid."[5]

So how may we avail ourselves of this new way of seeing? We have only to begin.

Usually most helpful if prayed in the quiet just before sleep, the Examen usually takes about a quarter of an hour and consists of five parts: first thanksgiving, then a prayer for illumination, next the examination of the day itself, followed by appropriate sorrow or delight, and finally, hope for the morrow.

1. "The first point is to give thanks to God our Lord for the benefits I have received" (43.2). In the first part of the prayer, one simply remembers that all we have and are belongs to God, who has loved us into being and will love us forever. It may well be, as the liturgy reminds us, "right always and everywhere to give God thanks and praise,"[6] but always and everywhere have a way of rushing past unrecognized. It is good to pause in our vulnerability on the rim of sleep, to rest into the amazing grace that surrounds us eternally. Specifically, we can give thanks for particular events or encounters or insights that the day has brought us as gifts. I have often been surprised to see what memories rise spontaneously to the surface of my mind in this first stage of the prayer; many times I have found myself delightedly saluting as pure gift a moment I would otherwise probably have completely forgotten.

2. "The second is to ask grace to know my sins and rid myself of them" (43.3). As preparation for the general overview of the whole day, one next prays simply for light, that God will enlighten our hearts. We ask for "grace to know"—and part of what that illuminating grace will reveal is, of course, the ways we have sinned. But we want to be open as well to an appreciation of the grace itself, an awareness of God authentically at work (and perhaps at play) in the day's events. Jesus promises that the Holy Spirit, whom the Father will send in his name, he "will teach you

all things, and bring to your remembrance all that I have said to you" (John 14:26 RSV). Day by day, if we consent to it, the Spirit will teach us more and more about God and about the ways we use God's gifts. I often imagine this teaching as what Julian of Norwich called "showings"—it is as though God directs the beam of a flashlight to reveal what otherwise might remain hidden from us. This part of the prayer is simply asking for that light.

3. "The third is to ask an account of my soul from the hour of rising to the present examen, hour by hour or period by period" (43.4, 5). This third part is the heart of the prayer, the examination of the day in the light of Christ, grounded in thankfulness for all that God has done for us. In my experience this is a bit as though God and I are sitting side by side watching clips of the day on videotape, from the moment I first woke up in the morning. It may be important to keep that somewhat detached view: As memories unwind, we are invited simply to watch them, not to leap in with judgments about ourselves or others. Too scrupulous or self-preoccupied an attention to our own failures and victories can miss the point as well. Remember we are not seeking so much to identify good and bad actions (to sort, label, and dismiss them as though taking an inventory in a shop) as to look beneath the actions to the desires and feelings that lie underneath (to discern how we have responded to God's loving presence in our lives).

For example, one might ask: In what I read today, or overheard on the bus, or saw in the evening news, was I drawn to God? Did I meet God in the joy or pain of others? Did I in some way bring Christ into my world? Did anyone bring God to me? Did I reach out to someone in trouble or sorrow? Did I omit or refuse to do so? Did something that happened to me today give me a keener sense of being loved, or being angry or tired, or needing God in some special way? Does any concrete event of the day reveal some part of my life that I am withholding from God? George Aschenbrenner, S.J., has pointed out, "In this third element of the examen we ordinarily rush to review, in some specific detail, our actions . . . so we can catalogue them as good or bad. Just what we shouldn't do! . . . *The operative questions are: what has been happening in us, how has the Lord been working in us, what has God been asking us*. And only secondarily are our own actions to be considered."[7]

Clearly, this form of prayer involves carefully and lovingly examining *everything* in the treasure chest, everything that been caught in the nets. This is no compelled/compulsive search for broken pieces to be rejected, but a prayerful exploration of *all* that the day contains in order to discover not only what is in need of healing but also what may have been neglected or ignored, or what might be celebrated.

4. "The Fourth is to ask pardon of God our Lord for my faults" (43.6). A quiet, honest look at the day from this perspective will lead naturally to both gratitude and sorrow. Particular memories of how we have responded (or failed to respond) to opportunities to see or to serve God may fill us with regret, and we will want to express to God how sorry we are. True awareness of our brokenness and blindness is in itself of course a gift granted in love, so at the same time we can give thanks for that. We can also—and this is very important—learn to see and be grateful for the ways in which we *were* able to rejoice in or witness to the love of God. Perhaps something marvelous has happened—we heard from an old friend, we reconciled with an old enemy, the kindness of a stranger reminded us of goodness alive in the world, a line in a song half-heard on the radio suddenly spoke to our heart.

There *will* be something in your day, a Jesuit friend of mine gently insists to people under his direction, that you can be proud of. "There will be things," he promises. "If you can't think of anything, then you haven't looked hard enough: don't move on before you think of what it might be. Then give thanks for this."[8] Even in the painful light of real sins named and offered to God's forgiving grace, we can marvel at the way God constantly brings us home and steadily leads us closer to becoming the people God means for us to be. The English poet Elizabeth Jennings muses:

> Prayer yet could be a dance
> But still a cross. I offer small heartbreak,
> Catch grace almost by chance.[9]

"Almost by chance"—but not quite, of course, not really. The grace we "catch" is steadily poured out for us in the clear and unshakable divine intention that we participate ever more fully in the very life of God.

For this reason, we need never lose hope.

5. "The Fifth is to resolve, with God's grace, to amend them" (43.7.). The final part of the Examen is to rest in that hope for the future. Tomorrow, like yesterday and today, is in God's hands. We can end our review of the day, our examination of our consciousness of God's activity in the ordinary events of our daily lives, by looking no longer back but ahead to the next day. Sometimes I end this final part of the prayer by recalling Paul's declaration: "One thing I do, forgetting what lies behind and straining forward to what lies ahead, I press on toward the goal for the prize of the upward call of God in Christ Jesus" (Phil 3:13-14). Sometimes I pray the prayer of St. Richard of Chichester: "May I know Thee more clearly, love Thee more dearly, and follow Thee more nearly, day by day."

Father Thomas Keating, the Cistercian monk who has introduced thousands to the method of "centering prayer," suggests that "our ordinary thoughts are like boats sitting on a river so closely packed together that we cannot see the river that is holding them up." The boats are not only crowded together, but they also pass by us quickly, and we become confused and distracted in our efforts to pay attention to the boats and what is on them. But the really important thing to see and understand is not the boats at all, but the river. When we enter deeply and quietly into prayer, Father Keating suggests, "space begins to appear between the boats. Up comes the reality on which they are floating."[10]

Very much the same dynamic is operative, I believe, in the Examen. As we allow God to draw our attention below the surface busyness, the color and activity of the boats, to the river itself, our hearts will be more and more deeply drawn into the fathomless reality of God. The purpose of the Examen is not simply to count the boats, or to judge either their condition or their cargo, but to get to know the river. The Examen, prayed deeply and faithfully, will enable us to take soundings, to learn the currents, to discern why the boats behave as they do. As we get to know the river, we will learn from experience that—for instance—staying too long in the shallows can be stagnating, that the ripples on the surface on a certain stretch warn of dangerous snags below, that if we go too fast in certain places we will collide with other boats.

The better we come to know the river, the easier it will be to see the subtle movement of God in our lives, and the more joyfully and fully we can cooperate with God's plans for us. The more authentically we "offer small heartbreak," the more grace we will "catch."

The more we pray the Examen, the more we will allow ourselves to be "transformed by the renewing of [our] minds, so that [we] may discern what is the will of God—what is good and acceptable and perfect" (Rom 12:2 NRSV).

Part 2:
Healing

– 7 –

Touched by God

A COUPLE OF YEARS AGO, the first harbingers of midlife hit me like a swarm of bees. Suddenly I was forced to stop and pay attention to my body. The attention I paid, at first, was angry, defensive, and ineffectual: Panicked, I swatted at the myriad stinging nuisances of hormonal upheaval, sleeplessness, back pain, headaches, and fatigue.

Impatiently I struggled against these evils—and I began to realize that, for many years, I had been treating my body as I treat my car: I acknowledge it as necessary to life as I know it; occasionally I remember to be grateful that I have it. But basically it is external, mechanical, subordinate to my "real" life, which I like to think is lived on the level of the spirit and the mind.

When my car requires maintenance or repair, I resent it. I expect my body, like my car, to operate smoothly and quietly—to get me where I want to go—but it had better be darned undemanding about it.

When my doctor first suggested that massage might relieve much of the lower back pain as well as reduce stress, and perhaps help with insomnia and headaches as well, I was dubious. It seemed a long shot—I was skeptical of "alternative medicine" and the whole new-age business of "body work"—and the process seemed dauntingly expensive both in money and time. But I was persuaded to try it. After all, when a mechanic I trust tells me my car needs an oil change or realignment, I may mutter rebelliously, but I take it in for the service it needs.

That was nearly two years ago. Since then, I have been receiving the benefits of regular therapeutic massage. It has promoted much healing not only in my aging, aching body but in the stiff joints of my theology and prayer as well.

As I allowed the skilled hands of the massage therapist to explore all the tension and pain I was carrying around in my body, I began to realize how carefully I had been carrying my religion in my head.

I was, in fact, surprised and humiliated to discover that I—a lifelong liberal Protestant, long accustomed to deploring the mind-body split fostered by wrong-thinking patriarchal theologians—had been nurturing a mind-body split within myself as deep and wide as the Grand Canyon.

The healing of this inner division came about gradually, almost imperceptibly at first. Integration occurred, as it so often does, completely by grace.

I had been praying the Scriptures early each morning as part of the Ignatian retreat in daily life I had been making, and had lately been meditating on the recurrent image of fishing nets in the Gospels. Peter and Andrew drop their nets to follow Jesus; the disciples cast their nets, pull in their nets. Especially, it had struck me, they mend their nets, frayed and torn by much hard use.

As I lay under a sheet on the massage table that day, meditating drowsily on the image of all those nets, Leah was methodically working her steel-fingered way down my spine. To my weary mind, her probing fingers seemed actually to be unhooking and reattaching each muscle to its vertebra. Something about the soothing repetition of the movement, and the sense of reconnecting muscle, bone, and tendon where they were meant to be, reminded me of watching my grandmother's crochet hook flash in and out of the afghans she was always either making or mending.

And then, in a flash, I knew myself to be a net, being mended. For a moment, it was Jesus' own hands I felt on my back, carefully reconnecting the places that had lost their moorings. I had never before permitted myself to imagine Jesus actually touching my body—my mind and heart, yes, of course; I spoke freely, even glibly, of being "touched" in that way—but really to feel the touch of Jesus on my skin was a revelation for me.

It was also a new thought that I, in my flesh and bones, might be valued by God. As valued as a fishing net, anyway. And wasn't that one of Jesus' commissioning promises to the disciples, that they would become "fishers of people"?

To the extent that I ever let myself think of myself as useful or precious to God, it was only because of my mind or my work or my words. Proper little gnostic that I had unconsciously become, I assumed that God valued only the "spiritual" in me.

But maybe—oh, revolutionary thought—Jesus was concerned about the mending and healing of my body as something he cared about, something he valued enough to mend when it was, like a fishing net, frayed by much hard use.

That was the beginning of the healing within me of the separation I had caused between my (unimportant) physical identity and my (important) intellectual and spiritual identity.

But it was only the beginning—God had only begun, that day, to heal my severed sense of self.

Another time, months later, in the midst of a massage, it occurred to me that Leah was kneading the muscles of my calf as though they were bread dough. All at once, spontaneously, I knew myself to be, in my body as well as in my mind, bread in the making, under God's kneading hands.

Without analyzing it or studying it—completely without benefit of commentary, concordance, or footnote—I knew in my bones that God was at work in me for my own transforming as surely as a woman who stirs a measure of yeast into her flour, a sacramental mystery as deep and as ordinary as bread on the table, bread on the altar, bread in the mouth.

And then again, just the other day, as Leah's discerning hands were loosening tension in my shoulders, I felt like clay in her hands—clay stiff and resistant at first, but surrendering in trust and gratitude to her shaping touch.

Instantly, the word of God came to me as it had to Jeremiah: "Behold, like the clay in the potter's hand, so are you in my hand" (18:6). Once again, I felt myself invited to appropriate the formative reality of God at the level of my body, in the reality of my clayness, deep in my bones.

The felt reality of God present in my life, creating, healing, shaping at the level of my bodilincss, has been a great gift to me in middle age. At this point, as never before, I know and feel myself to be in God's hands—not as a machine to be "fixed" but as a beloved, well-known creature: as earthy and tangible as a fishing net, as bread dough, as clay.

Finally, by the grace of God—by way of meditation and massage—I am beginning to be able, in body, mind and spirit, to honor the God who became flesh, at work and at home in my own flesh and bones.

– 8 –

Nursing Home Visit

Your arms, that lifted and carried
for so many, so long,
lie withered, useless, at your side.

Could you lift me into bed, you ask,
hating to ask, hating to be a bother.

Stricken with pity, awkward, I
bend over your shrunken body.

You lean your head against my neck
as simply as a child, and I lift
you from the chair in both my arms.

Your eyes are closed, your face is drawn
as I lay you down to sleep.

Have I hurt you, I whisper anxiously.
You smile, not speaking, not opening your eyes.

Suddenly, horribly, as I smooth
your faded hair and straighten out
the helpless legs my clumsiness has twisted,
I feel as though I'm laying out the dead.

As though I took you from a cross
instead of from a wheelchair.
Then I look upon that patient body,
worn with suffering, spent for others,

And realize perhaps I have.

– 9 –

Broken Pieces

In the Fractioning, We Are Made Whole

THE OTHER AFTERNOON I WAS SITTING AT MY DESK, typing an article I was late in finishing. The ribbon in my typewriter expired, and as I began the inky process of changing it, my nine-year-old daughter, Katie, called from her room: Could I help her with her homework "for just a second?" I left the ribbon half-changed and had no more than bent over her notebook when the telephone rang. As I was on the phone in the kitchen, my six-year-old, Emily, wandered in and asked for a snack. I hung up the phone, sliced an apple, poured milk, found crackers, and realized I had forgotten to thaw anything for dinner. Staring into the refrigerator, improvising a menu for four from its uninspiring contents, I heard Katie call, reproachfully, "Mom! What about my homework?"

On the way out of the kitchen, I wiped cracker crumbs off the counter, put milk on the shopping list, and made a note of the changed appointment time on the calendar. The calendar reminded me that a dozen books were overdue at the library, that the school rummage sale was this weekend, that I needed to arrange special transportation for Emily's dance class because Katie had an extra choir rehearsal on the same day, and that the deadline for the article I had only begun to type was now imminent. After I had untangled the knot of long division for Katie, I began once more to change the ribbon in my typewriter when the phone rang again.

And so it goes. The life I have chosen makes demands that fracture and splinter the days. Like Prufrock, I measure out my life in coffeespoons. There is not an unbroken moment. Even on good days, even the interruptions are interrupted. With Rilke I want to protest that "my life is not this steeply-sloping hour in which you see my hurrying"; but I am afraid that it is. Sometimes I am afraid that all my hours will steeply slope, that I will always be this hurried, this distracted. The burdens may be light, but they are many: Like Gulliver, bound by the Lilliputians with innumerable fine threads, I am immobilized by small things.

I can respond to all the myriad small demands each day presents only if I never stop moving. I can hold chaos at bay only by breaking each moment into as many pieces as possible, hoping almost desperately that there will be enough to go around, that I can spread myself thin enough to cover it all. Sometimes it feels not only as though time and strength and order are steadily eroded, but that somehow I am diminished as well; sometimes I feel myself disappearing.

How can I hope to achieve any of the serenity I crave, the wholeness I long for, in the midst of such tyrannous confusion?

I have begun to notice, in a rueful sort of way, how often Jesus in the Gospels seems as harried and distracted as a mother. He is forever trying to "get away to a quiet place" and is forever delayed and interrupted by the needs of other people, people he loves. Reading Matthew in the mornings lately, I am awed by Jesus' schedule, humbled by his patience and compassion.

I was particularly struck by the account of Jesus feeding the "great throng" that had "followed him on foot from the towns" (see Matt 14:13-21). With only five loaves and two fishes (less than even my much-raided refrigerator would yield on short notice), Jesus feeds a multitude. I have heard sermons on that text since I was a child. But what I realized recently for the first time was that by dividing, breaking up, and distributing that hastily gathered food, Jesus—so quietly, so casually—performed a miracle not of division but of multiplication. The gift of sustenance was not diminished but increased. Miracle indeed. Not a trick in my repertoire. In my experience, division only divides; fragmenting only fractures. Entropy rules.

Perhaps it is the endless shopping-cooking-serving labor of feeding my family that so draws me to the stories of Jesus feeding people. Perhaps it is my own need to be fed by Jesus that so draws me to the Eucharist. A family meal is at the center of the sacrament—bread broken, wine poured out.

At any rate, it was at the Eucharist that an insight was given me that may help in my struggle against the entropic forces that regularly disintegrate my life.

As I watched, the priest cast a practiced eye over the congregation and proceeded to break the consecrated wafer into a corresponding number of pieces. The perfect unblemished circle of the host was broken. First in half, then in half again, and then continuously divided, broken, fragmented, until it was reduced almost to crumbs. All that remained of its original integrity was a heap of fragments on the plate. "My life is like that," I realized.

I have long found a special grace in the orderly progression of the ritual that gathers and feeds us and sends us out. The bread and the cup lifted, blessed, and offered for us—our hearts lifted, blessed, and offered to God—all this has profound significance for me. The moments of Consecration and Communion are usually especially powerful.

But all at once, in my fatigue, it was not the Communion—bread shared in joyful company—that spoke to my condition, but the Fraction: bread broken; wholeness shattered; gift scattered. A feast diminished, reduced to crumbs that might be measured out in coffeespoons.

The difference, of course, between the Fraction of the host and the fraction of my days, is the difference between Christ's feeding of the multitude (by miraculous multiplication) and my own efforts (by laborious division) to nurture and hold together a family and a life.

When bread is broken in the sacrament, its strength is not diminished. I would never say that the tiny fragment of the host I receive in Communion is any less "profitable for my salvation" than the entire unbroken whole would be. In fact, in some mysterious way, by some gracious miracle of God, the strength is in the breaking and the breaking up.

I can see that the processes are similar: the wholeness of each God-given day reduced to a heap of broken moments; the wholeness of the host reduced to as many fragments as are required to feed the faithful. I can see that they are different: the weariness and discouragement at the end of my fragmented days; the strength and hope of wholeness that are given in the Eucharist. But I cannot see how to get there from here, how to bridge the gap between this disintegration and that integrity. No act of will, however Herculean, can transform my brokenness; no feat of time-management or jaw-clenched determination will ever turn my falling into rising, my mourning into dancing. Escalating my striving will not help.

Only grace provides in such abundance. Only love spreads such a feast. When, on that Galilean hillside, a multitude was fed with one child's picnic lunch, it was possible only because Jesus was there. In the sacrament, only the real presence of our risen Lord makes it possible for us to "keep the feast." In my own life, in my long days of breaking time into ever-smaller fragments so that there will be enough for every need, I can only hope for unity and peace if Christ is present. It is "in Christ"—perhaps only in Christ—that "all things hold together" (Col 1:17).

The fractioning of my days is not likely to end any time soon. But perhaps—by a miracle of grace, by the grace of God—I can come to see myself not as meaninglessly disintegrated but as broken and given like bread, poured out like wine. Maybe God will so enlighten the eyes of my heart (Eph 1:18) that I will come to see that all my time—no matter how broken and scattered—is in God's hand (Ps 31:15), a loving hand that also takes up "trouble and vexation" (Ps 10:14) and draws us "out of many waters" (Ps 18:16). There may even be such a miracle that I can come to see God present in small moments as surely as I find grace offered in a crumb at the Lord's table.

I cannot do this alone, but God can do it in me. No iron-fisted act of will can help me, but an act of faith might accomplish much. "O Lord, I am not worthy to receive you, but only say the word and I will be whole." I believe, with all my heart, that God longs to speak such a word, but that like the great lion Aslan in C. S. Lewis's Chronicles of Narnia, God "likes to be asked."

I suspect that silent prayer of aspiration, repeated throughout my hectic days, might in fact redeem the time—not that the breaking and the pouring out might end, but that they might be revealed to be sacramental; not so that my work will change to leisure, but that I might find God in the midst of it.

When bread is broken in the Eucharist, we do not rush to mend it. The celebrant does not attempt to fit the broken pieces back together again like Humpty Dumpty. The bread is meant to be broken, to be given and received, new each day, like manna in the wilderness. Perhaps each day, as well, is meant to be blessed and broken and given away. The broken pieces of my time may be (as in the sacrament) evidence not of failure but of love.

"Send us now into the world in peace, and grant us strength and courage to love and serve you, with gladness and singleness of heart, through Christ our Lord."[1] This final petition of the liturgy may hold the key: My life, my time, perhaps my heart, will be broken again and again, into ever-smaller pieces. But even the broken pieces may have meaning, may give strength. By the grace of God, through Christ our Lord, "gladness and singleness of heart" can still be ours for the asking—and the giving.

— 10 —

Do You Want to Be Healed?

WE ALL LONG TO BE CHANGED. Ancient traditions are brimful of songs and stories of metamorphosis, of transformation. We seem to be born with what the poet Emily Dickinson called "a dim capacity for wings."[1] Our culture notoriously capitalizes on that longing, pandering to our basic insecurities and insisting that we can be different (richer, smarter, healthier, more popular, stronger, more successful) if only we spend more money on self-improvement products and schemes. But far beneath that noisy, crowded, superficial level of our lives—the level accessible to Hollywood and Madison Avenue—our desire for transformation runs deep and strong as an underground river.

That desire is at the heart of our faith. It is the fundamental assumption of our sacramental theology: Baptism and Eucharist both speak to our yearning to be born again, to be remade, to become living members of the Body of Christ, to be part of the new creation. Our desire for God—and God's desire for us—is basic to our human nature and to our spiritual lives and is inextricably bound up with a desire to be changed.

Nevertheless, almost as deep in us as our yearning to be changed, to be delivered from "this body of death," is our resistance to our own transformation. Over and over again we lock God out, we cover our ears, we blind ourselves to the divine transformational opportunities that stand before us. I know at least that I, time and time again, pray for God to touch my life, to mend the brokenness within me, to be unambiguously present in my experience—and I think that I mean it, deeply, genuinely. But then—simultaneously—I so insist on my own way, miracles on my own terms, that I effectively remove myself from what might be my own rebirth. Like Eustace in C. S. Lewis's *The Voyage of the Dawn Treader*, I want to be undragoned, but I'd rather do it myself.

The story of the healing pool of Bethzatha in the Gospel of John (5:1-18) is a story of that kind of complicated longing, a yearning for wholeness that nonetheless almost doesn't see what has been offered, doesn't understand what has been given. In fact, that story is a fascinating glimpse into a couple of very different ways in which we sometimes block our awareness of God present with us and are so sure that we know what we need—and so sure of who and where God is—that we refuse to recognize our salvation when it stands directly in front of us.

Like so many of the Gospel accounts of Jesus healing someone, this passage tells of both miracle and resistance. An afflicted person is healed of his infirmity but seems almost not to realize it (and certainly not to realize who has done it). The religious authorities[2] are told the good news but see only the violation of the law. In this particular story, both the man healed of his disease and the Pharisees seem almost equally oblivious to the presence and the power of Jesus. And, I confess, the specifics of those parallel oblivions look pretty familiar to me: Like the afflicted man waiting for his freedom by the pool of Bethzatha, like the Pharisees attuned to the finest points of the law, I both seek my salvation and refuse to recognize it when it comes to me.

The first half of the text is a vivid, dramatic account of the miracle itself. The setting is a pool by the Sheep Gate in Jerusalem, surrounded by five porticoes, in the shelter of which lay "a multitude of invalids, blind, lame, paralyzed." They lay there waiting for the water to be "moved." Occasionally the still surface of the pool was disturbed, and whoever first stepped into the water after it had moved would be cured of whatever affliction he had. The man whom Jesus notices on this occasion had been lying there, ill and alone and helpless, for thirty-eight years: a lifetime in first-century Palestine. "When Jesus saw him and knew that he had been lying there a long time, he said to him, 'Do you want to be healed?' The sick man answered him, 'Sir, I have no man to put me into the pool when the water is troubled, and while I am going another steps down before me'" (John 5:6-7).

Imagine the man's hopelessness. Without a son or brother or

friend to carry him, he has no chance of being first, of getting to the healing water before someone else gets there ahead of him. For thirty-eight years he has been lying by the pool, watching others step broken into those angel-troubled waters and emerge whole, while he remains immobilized, isolated, year after year. Why has no one helped him in all that time? What has it done to him—what would it do to us—to be so close to those life-changing waters and never be able to reach them in time?

He does not answer Jesus' question. Does he simply ignore so self-evident a longing? Or has his desire to be first in some way actually replaced his desire to be well?

"Do you want to be healed?" Jesus asks him. In effect, the man answers, "I want to be first. For once, I want to be number one, to be at the head of the line, to have priority." Perhaps Jesus was the first person to speak to him in years. Perhaps the poor man saw an able-bodied young stranger with kind eyes and thought, "He might carry me down. This might be my chance." In any event, it is interesting to note that Jesus does not do (or offer to do, or explain why he is not doing) what the man expects him to do. Jesus does not lift the poor man into his strong arms and carry him to the waters—he bypasses altogether what custom and tradition require. He entirely omits, in fact, what the man is actually hoping for, the limited, human, practical compassion that is all the fellow can imagine, and more than—in nearly forty years—he has received.

As I imagine this scene, Jesus crouches down to speak with the man, who is lying on his pallet, flicking only one anxious glance at Jesus before returning his restless eyes to the pool, estimating his chances, cursing his helplessness, gauging the crowd, looking for someone to help him. In my imagination, Jesus' back is to the water; his whole attention is focused not on what the man sees or wants but on the man himself. As far as we can tell from the story, the man doesn't ever "get it"—and Jesus doesn't insist on his understanding. Jesus so easily could have said, "Look at me: I can make you whole and strong—only trust in me, and not in the magic water. All you need is me; you do not need to be first." But instead, Jesus said to the man, " 'Rise, take up your pallet, and walk.' And at once the man was healed, and he took up his pallet and walked" (John 5:8-9).
Once again, as so often in the Gospel miracle stories, Jesus heals an afflicted person so quietly and unobtrusively that if we blink, we miss

it. This time there is no laying on of hands, no touching, no prayers. Just "Rise." Stand up from this long dying. Walk away from the pool that has disappointed you so many times. You are well, you are whole, you have received your miracle. And it came from a source you never imagined. The Gospel does not indicate that the man paused to thank Jesus or to praise God for his healing. It does not appear that Jesus pointed out just what had happened. Jesus does not seem to have needed to be recognized—or to have the man understand that the wholeness God meant for him had nothing at all to do with being first.

All Jesus did was make him well and slip unnoticed into the crowd. Later, it seems, Jesus sought the man out and spoke to him again. "Now the man who had been healed did not know who it was, for Jesus had withdrawn, as there was a crowd in the place. Afterward, Jesus found him in the temple, and said to him, 'See, you are well!'" (John 5:13-14) What Jesus risked by that affectionate greeting was exactly what happened: The man who had been healed, upon realizing who had made him well, on recognizing Jesus for who he was, went and identified him to the religious authorities who were seeking to persecute him for healing on the Sabbath.

This brings us to the second part of the story, the response of the Pharisees to the realization that Jesus had brought healing to a man who had been afflicted for thirty-eight years. The authorities, like the lame man, resist the wholeness Jesus offers, are blind to the miracle of his transforming presence—not out of helplessness or hopelessness but out of a religious legalism that cannot bear grace that does not play by the rules. This specific form of resistance to God, I must confess, feels uncomfortably familiar to me. Trained in law myself, it is all too easy for me to identify with the law-abiding determination that the Sabbath restrictions be enforced in all particulars. Raised as a Presbyterian, brought up to reverence "decency and order" as gospel values, it is all too easy for me to imagine outrage at the sight of a man heedlessly performing a clearly prohibited task, apparently showing no respect at all for the law or for the holiness of the Sabbath. Therefore, it is especially troubling to see how Jesus deals with the authorities compared to the way he encountered the lame man. There is no tenderness here, no patient compassion, no half-amused solicitude. There is, in this passage, no healing for those who insist on their own way. "You search the scriptures because you think that in them you have eternal life; . . . yet you refuse to come to me that you may have life" (John 5:39-40).

There are, it seems, ways of opposing God that are more dangerous to our own salvation than others. The afflicted man may have been, as Raymond Brown suggests, unimaginative, crotchety, dull, and naive[3]—he may have failed to recognize Jesus and his marvelous invitation into wholeness of life—but he did accept and receive the healing Jesus offered. The religious authorities, on the other hand, seem to have been not so much impoverished and afflicted as too full of themselves and their own importance to see their own poverty and affliction. (Sometimes, Simone Weil reminds us, we are in danger of starving to death not because there is no bread but because we think we are not hungry.[4]) To insist on obedience to authority rather than receptivity to grace—to be so determined to be in the right that we cannot even tell when we are in the dark—this is a terrible way to keep God out of our lives.

Attachment to our own grievances and expectations ("I never get to be first; there is no one to help me") can act as a powerful barrier to the abundant life God longs to give us. Even more perilously, we can become so attached to our own need to be right and to be in control ("How dare you challenge my authority? How can you presume to know God in ways I have not approved?") that we place ourselves outside the longing for change that might lead us toward God.

First, we must yearn for this change. We must know the depths of our need before we will be able to hear Jesus asking us, "Do you want to be healed?"

– 11 –
Wounded and Healed

JESUS HAS ALWAYS HAD a remarkable attraction not only for the sick and the poor but for those who are, in the words of the Book of Common Prayer, "in danger, sorrow, or any kind of trouble."[1] The New Testament is crowded with people in pain of all kinds and degrees, seeking a healing encounter with one they intuitively know can make them whole. Jesus can, and does. In the Gospel stories, transforming love pours out of Jesus like water from from a spring, restoring health and vision and quietness of mind.

This is, as my Sunday school teachers used to tell us, a great mystery. An even greater mystery is that Jesus *continues* to pour his healing power into our broken lives, not only two millennia after his terrible death but somehow precisely because of it. "By his wounds you have been healed," we are promised (1 Pet 2:24). We are, in Christ, made whole not despite his own woundedness but by means of it.

This apparently essential connection between Christ's brokenness and our wholeness, this paradox of weakness and strength, is at the heart of our faith. Exploring this mystery can reveal much not only about the nature of God but about the meaning of our own pain and the graced possibilities even within unhealed wounds.

I was present once at a Mass where the celebrant was deaf: I was deeply moved by the beauty and authority with which the priest signed the entire liturgy, like a dance to silent music, giving "new meaning to the word made flesh."[2] I learned that day that the signed name for Jesus is two taps in the palm of each hand, indicating the marks of the nails. Jesus Christ is—essentially—the wounded One; his wounds tell us who he is.

I think St. Thomas would have appreciated that signature; I believe the nature of Thomas' famous "doubting" is often misunderstood. "Unless I see the marks of the nails," he declared (to his brethren to whom, incidentally, Jesus had already shown his pierced hands and side), "I will not believe." I have never been able to assume that Thomas was doubting that Christ was risen, or that he was skeptical that the disciples were speaking the truth of their own experience. I think he was merely insisting that any alleged appearance of his Lord that did not bear the marks of his suffering could not be authentic. If he were not manifestly the one who had suffered, Thomas really may have been saying, then he cannot be the Risen One. When Thomas saw Jesus, he knew: "My Lord and my God," he recognized him.

This is the mystery at the crux of the matter, this suffering love that is transformed by death but not annihilated by it; that still, even in victory, bears the marks of the nails. This saving truth is so much a part of God that it has become God's name. This is the Paschal mystery. And it is more than abstract mystical theology; it is a living reality available to each one of us. When Jesus freely accepted a terrible death, he redeemed our dying, transfigured (but did not annihilate) all our pain. There is nothing we can suffer that Christ does not know, has not shared, cannot somehow use in love, with us, for the healing of the world.

Pain and grief as integral to human experience is a grim reality richly attested to in Scripture. The psalms, for instance, are full of the anguish of God's people, who have been fed "with the bread of tears," given "bowls of tears to drink."[3] The mothers' inconsolable sorrow for the children killed by Herod echoes the bitter woe of Rachel, "weeping for her children." The Bible does not flinch from this ancient darkness, as we at the dawn of the new millennium have been conditioned to do—denying the harsh inevitability of pain, anesthetizing our minds, pretending that it's not so bad, that things will inevitably be better soon.

Frodo Baggins, the reluctant hero of Tolkien's *Lord of the Rings* trilogy, did not delude himself with such shallow optimism: by the end of his adventures, Frodo is indeed victorious over the enemies of Middle Earth, but he has been painfully and irretrievably wounded in his costly battles with the evil ones. His injuries are mortal; he realizes that there is no healing for them in this world. But Frodo faces his remaining life and eventual death with a quiet and a valiant heart, trusting that wholeness will be restored in the "far green country under a swift sunrise," where "the sound of singing comes over the water."[4] Our more facile notion of healing as "fixing," rather than as a surrender to God so total as to be a kind of dying, has hidden this deep hope from us.

Other centuries have been wiser. The sixteenth century, for example, when the Black Death was a terrible reality for many, has given us an almost unbearably profound image of Christ in his woundedness. In 1516 Matthias Grunewald painted what is now known as the Isenheim Altarpiece for the hermits of St. Anthony, who cared for victims of the plague. In the central crucifixion panel of this work, the figure of Christ on the Cross is enormous, twice the size of his companions. Christ's suffering is graphic and grotesque. His flesh is green, covered with festering sores; his face and limbs are contorted with agony. Grunewald has, in fact, depicted Christ as dying of the plague. In the foreground (lest we miss the meaning) is a lamb, its eyes on Jesus, bleeding from a cut in its breast into a chalice. The message is starkly clear: In the bleeding wounds of Christ lie our hope and our salvation.

The men and women who died with this image before them five hundred years ago were not cured of the plague by their faith in Christ, who suffered with them. They were not spared the horrors of that death, did not have their mortal illness "fixed" or eliminated by the crucified one, any more than Jesus escaped his own end. They did, however, have the transforming opportunity not only to know themselves companioned by Christ crucified but also to experience their death as radical healing.

Dying with and into Christ, they could hope to rise with him, could hope with St. Paul that having carried in their bodies the death of Jesus, the life of Jesus might also be manifested in them. Death was consciously for them (as it remains for us, consciously or not) the doorway into fullness of life. Somehow, entry into Christ's woundedness is entrance into Eternity.

There is another medieval witness to this revealed truth in the shape of a Latin prayer still beloved around the world, the *Anima Christi*, or "Soul of Christ." One line of this prayer has traditionally been translated as "within thy wounds hide me"—implying, astonishingly to our modern minds, that Christ's wounds are not only a source of healing but a kind of shelter. Within the embrace of Christ's wounds lies our only refuge, and our hope of glory only on the other side.

Most of us at the beginning of the twenty-first century will not face death from the plague, but we will all face death. And even in this life, as we know to our sorrow, there are wounds that do not heal. There are losses that are not recoverable. Life seems to give each of us, at one time or another, bowls of tears to drink.

An old friend and I were talking once about the deep sorrows in our lives, some of which we have in common. I confessed to him that despite the passage of many years, I found resolution elusive: Two or three wounds were so deep I feared they would never heal. My friend nodded gravely, compassionately. Then, "That's actually pretty good, Deborah," he responded. "Only three unhealed wounds? You are luckier than most."

C. S. Lewis wrote *A Grief Observed* as a kind of journal after the death of his beloved wife. In its pages, Lewis speculates on the nature of devastating loss and the limits of recovery. It is one thing to "get over" the flu or an appendectomy, but how does one "get over" an amputation, he wonders: After that operation either the wounded stump heals or the man dies. If it heals, the fierce, continuous pain will stop. Presently he'll get back his strength and be able to stump about on his wooden leg. He has 'got over it.' But he will probably have recurrent pains in the stump all his life, and perhaps pretty bad ones; and he will always be a one-legged man."[5]

There are some losses, Lewis reminds us, that change and diminish us forever, that can never be "got over." Even the consolations of our faith can only go so far. Pondering the limits of religious comfort, Lewis wonders about a mother who has lost a child:

> If a mother is mourning not for what she has lost but for what her dead child has lost, it is a comfort to believe that the child has not lost the end for which it was created. And it is a comfort to believe that she herself, in losing her chief or only natural happiness, has not lost a greater thing, that she may still hope to "glorify God and enjoy Him forever." A comfort to the God-aimed, eternal spirit within her. But not to her motherhood. The specifically maternal happiness must be written off. Never, in any place or time, will she have her son

on her knees, or bathe him, or tell him a story or plan for his future, or see her grandchild.[6]

For Lewis, the transforming insight in his own grief and loneliness was not a glib assurance that he would get over his shattering loss but the firm conviction that God had not left him alone in his sorrow. Presence, not "recovery," was what enabled him to believe again that "all shall be well."[7]

All of us can, at times, identify with St. Paul, who "three times besought the Lord" to remove the unspecified torment of the "thorn in the flesh." Paul's plea was refused. Christ told him, "My grace is sufficient for you, for my power is made perfect in weakness" (2 Cor 12:9). Paul chose to accept his weakness "that the power of Christ may rest upon" him, learning to be content with calamities for the sake of Christ.

Paul learned to live and die, as Frodo did, as many of us may be called to do, with the thorn in place, the wound unhealed—trusting that, in ways beyond our understanding or imagining, God does somehow, in all things, work for good, and that there is no tribulation or distress that can separate us from God. As Michael Mayne has written, "Our most painful human wounds are most intimately connected to the sufferings of God himself, for in Christ [God] . . . knows . . . what it is to live, to know pain at its potentially most destructive, to face desolation and to die."[8]

As we may all have St. Paul's experience of a thorn in the flesh (or the heart or the mind), so we all have his freedom to accept with serenity the pain he could not leave behind. As Viktor Frankl learned from his experience of the death camps, when we cannot change our circumstances, we are nonetheless free to determine our response to them, seeking meaning in the calamitous losses and torments our lives may hold. "It is this spiritual freedom—which cannot be taken away—that makes life meaningful and purposeful."[9]

The alternative may be freely chosen also, alas: Instead of accepting the invitation to join our deepest sorrows to Christ's, instead of seeking shelter within his wounds and meaning in our suffering, instead of permitting Christ's strength to be made perfect in our weakness, we can (and all too often do) allow our own suffering merely, meaninglessly, to devour us.

Emily Dickinson, in one of her poems, refers to the death of an unidentified "great hope" and her attempt to deny this devastating loss. She realizes, however, that "not admitting of the wound" had dangerously enlarged it "until it grew so wide that all my Life had entered it."[10]

This is the terrible possibility inherent in our pain: that it remains forever merely pain, unadmitted, unshared. Enlarged, but to make a dead end, not a doorway into life; opened large only to swallow the rest of ourselves, as the black holes in the universe are said to swallow light itself.

Suffering does not always lead to compassion: Our wounds, if they have been long neglected or denied, can fester, can compromise our ability to respond to others. But Christ's woundedness is not like that. He suffered on our behalf, and in the power of the Resurrection, he can change all our sorrows into part of that same miracle of love. In Christ, and with him and through him, supported by his own courage, humility, and trust, we need only to "admit the wound" and our own helplessness to heal it. Then even our most mortal wounds can become the doors by which we enter life.

Perhaps this is a part of what Jesus meant when he said, "I am the door" (John 10:9), when he promised, "Behold, I have set before you an open door, which no one is able to shut" (Rev 3:8). Christ's wounds are the doorway into our life in him, offering us both shelter and opportunity, both refuge and a new beginning. Our whole lives—unhealed wounds and broken hearts and all—can enter by that door and be redeemed.

But the promise is even more wonderful than that. Our wounds, when blessed by God, can also be a source of healing for others. Henri Nouwen speaks of this sacramental possibility in *The Wounded Healer*, reminding us that we are charged to be honest with each other, admitting the pain and vulnerability within us, putting the suffering of our own lives at the disposal of the larger community. This "does not call for a sharing of superficial personal pains," Nouwen explains, "but for a constant willingness to see one's own pain and suffering as rising from the depth of the human condition."[11] As Christians, Nouwen claims, we are called to be "articulate witnesses of Christ," allowing others to "enter our lives" even through the doorways of our own wounds.[12] The same courage, humility, and trust that will help us to enter Christ's transforming woundedness will help us in turn to lead others to their own difficult dyings-into-Christ.

I once heard a wise priest say, in a meditation on gratitude, that we should be especially grateful for whatever breaks our hearts.[13] Reflecting on God's promise to write "upon" our hearts rather than "within" them, he suggested that our own hearts are so hard that all God can do is write upon the surface. It is only when our hearts break that they break open; then the word of God can enter deeply, like a seed in a harrowed field.

Perhaps this heartbroken availability is the "gift of tears" the desert fathers prized so highly and urged each other to seek so urgently: "Before all else, pray to be given tears, that weeping may soften the savage hardness which is in your soul."[14] As George Maloney has put it, "The hard shell of self-containment must be split open" before we can be truly healed, or truly compassionate.[15] A penitential life of disciplined prayer may lead to the grace of being broken open in this way, and as Gregory of Nyssa reminds us, "it is impossible for one to live without tears who considers things exactly as they are."[16] But in a special mercy, not only the specifically prayed-for tears of the ascetics will avail us this vision and this ministry; the ordinary sorrows of an ordinary life will suffice.

None of this would be possible, of course, if our God were not the wounded one, who out of unimaginable love for the world is "a man of sorrows, and acquainted with grief" (Is 53:3 RSV).

In a poignant moment in C. S. Lewis's Narnia Chronicles, the young boy Digory is heartbroken by the realization that his mother is dying and that he can do nothing to save her. He raises his despairing face to the great lion Aslan and is startled to see "great shining tears" in Aslan's eyes. "They were such big, bright tears compared with Digory's own that for a moment he felt as if the Lion must really be sorrier about his Mother than he was himself. 'My son, my son,' said Aslan, 'I know. Grief is great. Only you and I in this land know that yet. Let us be good to one another.'"[17]

Digory chooses to trust Aslan, although the sacrifice of his hopes and plans is so terrible that it is a kind of death. Obedient to Aslan's instructions for the protection of newly created Narnia, Digory sets off on a journey to pluck an apple from a tree in the center of a garden at the top of a green hill, returning to Aslan untasted and unstolen the apple that might, so the Witch had told him, have saved his mother. "He was very sad and he wasn't even sure all the time that he had done the right thing: but whenever he remembered the shining tears in Aslan's eyes he became sure."[18]

The rest of Digory's adventures are too long to relate here, but in the end his long faithfulness is rewarded, Narnia is protected from evil, and his mother's life is saved, although not in the way he had imagined he desired. In the process, Digory's sense of what it is to heal and be healed is itself transformed. And so it can be with us. If we surrender our own limited vision of what our healing might be, if we can accept that presence is worth more than "recovery," we may be amazed at what God has in mind for us.

This may not be "healing" as the world sees it: Our losses may remain nearly intolerable; our betrayals may grieve us till we die. But to bear such unhealed wounds with courage and trust and generosity of spirit is to live close to the heart of God and to live toward the promised day of resurrection, whose joys no eye has seen nor human heart imagined.

— 12 —

Grief on Ice

I haven't been on skates in twenty years.
It feels incongruous now—this
birthday party gaiety, when
grief stuns me; tears unshed
make my throat ache,
my head swim.
I strike out bravely across the rink
and falter, take
a wrong step, stop.
I bend, blinded by sorrow,
to fumble with a lace.

The loss of you. So long feared,
so many times denied.
Now, despite our desperate longings,
your loss upon us
an appalling darkness,
blotting out the sun.

What shall we do, I wonder,
collapsed upon the ice
over my rented skate, undone.
Go round in circles
of artificial winter
till we all run down?

Only the cold is real.
I remember other winters.
Rivers locked in death.

At least the sun shone then.
The ice was rough, the bitter breath
of snow was hard upon our faces,
but we were young—
not only the cold was real.
We linked our mittened hands
and sped laughing toward the
setting sun. Invincible.

Now I am forty and felled by sorrow
in a foreign place.

Strangers pass me.
The ice beneath our feet is thin,
and overlays cement.
No river murmurs here,
no hidden depths
move dark among the roots of trees.

I mourn your loss,
the loss of hope, and youth,
and waters that run underneath.

I crouch, miserable,
weeping among strangers,
a broken skate lace in my fingers.

And then
for an instant
you are there
a fleeting touch
a laughing shout
and you are past me
waving.

Whole and free and strong.
Most real, most living.
I stand, wondering,
and shade my eyes with
a mittened hand against the sun
as you disappear,
upriver,
into light.

Part 3:
Spiritual Companionship

— 13 —

No Greater Love

Reclaiming Christian Friendship

THE AUGUST CHRISTIAN DISCIPLINE of spiritual direction—for centuries an important aspect of religious life, especially in the monastic tradition—is being hailed as good news from a far country by many of us outside the Roman Catholic Church. Suddenly Protestant ministers are being urged explicitly to undertake the spiritual direction of their flocks as a hitherto neglected form of pastoral care; laypeople hungry for guidance are seeking directors as, in another decade, they might have sought gurus in India or "EST" in California.

A host of books on the practice of spiritual direction has been published in recent years; many seminaries are providing whole new curricula, certification programs, even advanced degrees toward this rediscovered "specialization in professional ministry."

It has even become politically correct in certain mainline circles not only to "have" a director of one's own, but to be able (discreetly) to produce the fact as a kind of trump card on occasion, particularly if one has been clever enough to acquire a director of the really right sort: certainly a vowed Roman Catholic religious, preferably female, optimally of famously rigorous order—a Carmelite prioress is ideal.

Unfortunately, Carmelite prioresses are in rather short supply. The situation created by this sudden demand for a limited commodity—by this fashionable enthusiasm for a little understood form of relationship—has troubling implications, not only for what one might call the religious market economy but also for the Church's working definitions of community, authority, and love.

Let me hasten to say that, as a fully engaged and deeply ecumenical Protestant laywoman, I applaud the new interest in the responsi-

ble formation of the people of God. For far too long the Reformed tradition has tended to brandish the Calvinist dictum that "God alone is Lord of the conscience" to defend a deeply rooted suspicion of personal piety in any save a missionary expression. The sad result has been that whole generations of the Calvinist faithful, dimly aware of an inner call to deeper union with the Holy, have had to struggle more or less alone and unaided to nourish their primary relationship with God.

"Worship" was what happened on Sunday morning; "prayer," aside from family grace before meals, was what the clergy did for us. Justification was by faith alone, which became an excuse for ignoring or deriding as "pietistic" any instinct for personal religion. *Scriptura sola* meant that the treasures of the mystics have been either suspect or unknown. In the last twenty years Protestant denominations have secularized and psychologized spiritual concerns to such an extent that a referral to a therapist or a twelve-step program is often the best we feel we can offer people whose essential hunger may be for guidance in prayer.

Given this impoverished and impoverishing attitude toward prayer and a God-centered life, the notion that help is available, that trained spiritual direction is possible, is in fact good news. (I should also—modestly—add that I have benefited in the last decade more than I can say from the lion heart and eagle eye of my own director, who happens to be a Roman Catholic sister in a famous order, although she is not now nor has she ever been a Carmelite prioress.)

So on the one hand I rejoice to see the sometimes narrow Protestant view of personal religion enlarged by the richness of the Catholic mystical and monastic traditions of individual spiritual formation. The central insight, it seems to me, is not only sound but obvious: As Evelyn Underhill pointed out, when one is exploring the high country, one needs a guide who knows the mountain.

Nevertheless, I am made uneasy by the unreflective speed with which Protestants are adopting unexamined assumptions about the nature of growth in Christ and about the extent to which such growth is impossible without benefit of clergy.

Kenneth Leech, whose book *Soul Friend*[1] was a groundbreaking text on the ministry of spiritual direction when it was first published in 1977, has recently declared himself alarmed about the "potentially extremely dangerous" way in which spiritual direction is being

professionalized and seen as a specialist's ministry and about the degree to which institutes, networks, and international organizations have sprung up to accommodate the current interest in training spiritual directors.[2]

In a time when feminist and lay reflections on the nature and structure of ministry are beginning to be heard, it seems a pity not to use those insights to evaluate some of the assumptions that underlie the traditional forms of (as well as current trends in) spiritual direction. I do not mean merely, as is often said, that it is sometimes both overly "spiritual" and excessively "directive," although I agree with Margaret Guenther[3] and Kathleen Fischer[4] that that is often the case, to the detriment of women's experience and in perpetuation of exclusively hierarchical models of the religious life.

My present uneasiness stems more from a concern that emerging patterns of the director/directee relationship (as it is being promoted by some Protestant seminaries and churches) tend to support an already problematic view of ministry—one that is overly clerical and overly professional and that implicitly denies the sacramental value of ordinary friendship.

I suggest that the present openness to the importance of "personal religion" in the life of Reformed churches might be a window of opportunity in more ways than one. Perhaps in addition to appropriating the wisdom of the Roman Church's long experience of spiritual direction, Protestants might do well to consider exploring some perspectives other than the traditional "confessional" model, with all its powerful if unspoken assumptions about the superiority of vowed, celibate life. There might be benefit as well in reclaiming some of the implicit promises of Reformation understandings of mutual accountability, community discipline, and the priesthood of all believers.

Specifically, I hope that we can all, Protestants and Catholics alike, reexamine the marvelous possibilities inherent in authentic and responsible Christian friendship.

The idea of friendship as a positive agent in religious life has not, of course, historically been seen as an unmixed blessing by church authority. "Particular friendships" were notoriously forbidden in the monastic novitiate, for example, and until quite recently Catholic schoolchildren were routinely warned that "where two are gathered together, the Devil makes a third." Even my own thoroughly Protestant upbringing was vigilantly supervised to prevent both intimate friendships *à deux* and (even worse) solitude. The jocund group was the thing; "fellowshipping" was a labor-intensive activity.

Nevertheless, there is a strand of the tradition that, from the beginning, has seen friendship between Christians as a "means of grace" and a reflection of our "hope of glory." Aelred of Rievaulx is perhaps the most famous proponent of the value of "spiritual friendship." His twelfth-century treatise, *Spiritual Friendship*, is a classic on the subject and a gem of a book, startling, poignant, and persuasive.[5]

Aelred, a popular young nobleman in the royal court of Scotland, became a much-loved Cistercian abbot and seems to have had a personal genius for intimate friendship. But it was not merely his own temperament and experience that led him to hold friendship in such high regard. *Spiritual Friendship* is, among other things, a variation on a theme articulated earlier by the philosopher Cicero, which Aelred adapts for the purposes of a committed Christian life, also drawing powerfully on Scripture and St. Augustine's *Confessions*.

That Aelred's view of friendship is exalted is evident throughout. Great claims are made, in hyperbolic terms, identifying spiritual friendship among Christians with the perfect love of God so explicitly that he can go so far as to suggest that "God is friendship."[6] Aelred refers all human friendship to Christ: The friendship that ought to exist between us "begins in Christ, is preserved according to the spirit of Christ, and . . . its end and fruition are referred to Christ."[7] (Interestingly, two centuries later Thomas à Kempis would insist on the same groundedness in Christ, putting in Christ's own mouth the warning that "your love for a friend must rest in Me, and those who are dear to you in this life must be loved only for My sake. No good and lasting friendship can exist without Me.")[8]

Aelred goes on to claim that friendship is in fact indispensable to the abundant life: "Among the stages leading to perfection, friendship is the highest."[9] "We have nothing better from God," he declares.[10] A life without friendship is hardly human at all: "Scarcely any happiness whatever can exist . . . without friendship, and a man is to be compared to a beast if he has no one to rejoice with him in adversity, no one to whom to unburden his mind . . . or with whom to share some unusually sublime or illuminating inspiration. . . . He is entirely alone who is without a friend."[11]

Aelred's tone occasionally reveals his debt to courtly forms of friendship (as his pronouns reveal his assumptions about the gender of his readers), but he is, essentially, neither sentimental nor romantic. On the contrary, he is, to modern ears, ferociously exacting and alarmingly demanding in his guidelines for "'that friendship which is spiritual and therefore true."[12] True friendship will be stable[13] and eternal.[14] It must be entered into carefully, with a mode of selection and a period of testing that sound remarkably like a novitiate. Most significantly, perhaps, true Christian friends (once selected, and tested, and admitted to real intimacy and trust) have enormous responsibility for each other, zealously to guard each other's good and fearlessly to admonish each other's error.

Aelred writes: "Let friend counsel friend as to what is right, securely, openly, and freely. And friends are not only to be admonished, but if necessity arises, reproved as well. For although truth is offensive to some . . . yet complacency is far more hurtful, because it indulges in wrongdoing and thus suffers a friend to be borne headlong to ruin."[15] This deep and courageous loyalty presupposes the supreme standard of the sacrificial love of God and echoes Jesus' own words: "No one has greater love than this, to lay down one's life for one's friends" (John 15:13 NRSV).

This is a high view of friendship—high and deep and wide and glorious. And perhaps particularly corrective for us in the world today. Ours is a culture that, intending to celebrate individual freedom and religious tolerance, instead promotes loneliness and isolation, and effects superficiality, impermanence, and self-interest in human relationships.[16] Possibly friendship is not taken seriously these days as a real element in spiritual growth not because it is felt to be too dangerous to a holy life but because it is too weak to be a factor at all. Our sense of what can be expected, hoped for, or relied on among friends is far from Aelred's.

Nevertheless, his is not an impossible vision for us today—especially of course as we, no less than the medieval Cistercian community at Rievaulx, have the support of the Holy Spirit to preserve and sustain all our relationships. In fact, I am convinced that the recovery of an Aelredian sense of the value of true companionship among Christians would go far to address the apparently critical lack of good spiritual directors. In friendship, I believe, we may find a model for the Body of Christ as a living reality—a model for community, authority, prophecy, discernment, and the all-claiming love of God.

At the heart of the Christian life is the relationship between ourselves and God. That relationship—which Leslie Weatherhead has called "the transforming friendship"—is an intimate, ultimate, passionate connectedness that is sustained by endless grace and costly discipline, that implies risk and vulnerability and trust at the deepest levels, that dares to affirm that "unto God all hearts are open, all desires known, from [God] no secrets are hid."[17] That profound, covenanted mutuality—the "I and Thou" of our primary relationship with God—is a gift and a promise that extend to all of us in baptism and is (or might be!) the ground of all our relationships. Aelred sums this up with beautiful simplicity in the opening sentence of *Spiritual Friendship:* "here we are, you and I, and I hope a third, Christ, is in our midst."[18]

This is the deep union for which Jesus prays for his disciples: "that they may be one, even as we are one . . . , that the love with which thou hast loved me may be in them, and I in them" (John 17:11, 26). These are high claims indeed, referring human community and human relationships not only to the love that binds any soul to its Creator but also to the great mystery of the love between the Father and the Son, that dynamic uncreated unity from which all creation springs.

We are accustomed to seeing certain kinds of human love as aspiring to that life-giving height and depth: the bond between a mother and her child, for instance, or between a woman and a man in an extraordinary marriage. But Aelred suggests—and Jesus commanded—that much more of human experience than the maternal or the conjugal be intentionally rooted and grounded in love.

> This is my commandment, that you love one another as I have loved you. No one has greater love than this, to lay down one's life for one's friends. You are my friends if you do what I command you. I do not call you servants any longer, . . . but I have called you friends, because I have made known to you everything that I have heard from my Father. . . . I am giving you these commands so that you may love one another. (John 15:12-15, 17 NRSV)

"I have called you friends," Jesus said. What might it mean if we took seriously and joyfully the privilege of being his friends, and of being friends with each other in the same way?

One of the most immediately striking implications is obedience: "You are my friends *if you do what I command you.*" Another is costliness: "Love one another *as I have loved you.*" Whatever else it may be, Christian friendship is no facile matter of tolerant amiability or even gregarious solicitude. Christian friendship, as Alan Jones has observed, "is for the healing of the world."[19] Moreover, it "is a much tougher and more resilient relationship than is often supposed."[20] Where such Christian friendship is found, it will be characterized by reciprocal honesty and accountability, mutual support, and an attentive shared communion in the mystical Body of Christ.

Interestingly, much of what Scripture has to say about friendship assumes this kind of toughness: Hearts and flowers are conspicuous by their absence in maxims such as "Iron sharpens iron, and one man sharpens another" (Prov 27:17), or "Faithful are the wounds of a friend; profuse are the kisses of an enemy" (Prov 27:6). Part of what it means to be a friend, it seems, is a risky and courageous determination to hold each other to account, a willingness not only to nurture and support but to confront and challenge.

Aelred, as has already been noted, is quite clear on this point: "Friends are not only to be admonished, but if necessity arise, to be reproved as well."[21] Easy tolerance of dangerous behavior or reluctance to appear interfering or judgmental has no place in true friendship, Aelred would insist. No true friend will avoid the unpleasant necessity of reproving a friend lest "the friend be borne headlong to ruin."[22]

This, presumably, is where "iron sharpens iron." Being faithful to each other requires strength, even a kind of resistant hardness on occasion, a willingness to shout "Beware!" if we perceive a friend to be in mortal danger. Of course, this role in moral or spiritual crisis is classically the role of the prophet in the community. St. John of the Cross assigned this prophetic role, under the charism of discernment of spirits, to the superior of the monastery; John Calvin similarly charged the kirk session with its solemn duty to warn the recalcitrant against the impenitent reception of the sacraments. It is also, perhaps, a natural role of any intimate friendship. However, as the Catholic hermit Maggie Ross reminds us, friendship too frequently shrinks from the prophetic role, and as a result, discernment amounts to little more than "If it feels good, do it." As Robert McAllister, an American Jesuit, has pointed out, "Everyone at some time needs the strength of a friend who says, Please don't do that; it is not good for you."[23]

We are not accustomed to speaking of the "prophetic role" in friendship, but it is interesting to note that Aelred does not hesitate to do so. "Indeed a man owes truth to a friend, without which the name of friendship has no value."[24] In fact, Aelred assumes difficult truth-telling in friendship to a rather breathtaking degree. He calmly commends the prophet Nathan not for his audacity in confronting King David with his own murder and adultery but for the "prudence" with which Nathan "extracted from the king himself a judgment against his own person."[25] (The reference, of course, is to Nathan's famous parable of the ewe lamb, to which the indignant king responds by declaring that "the man who has done this deserves to die," only to have Nathan implacably pronounce, "You are the man.")[26]

If, as Alan Jones has suggested, one of the purposes of the spiritual life is that we hold up mirrors for each other that we may better see ourselves as we really are, then perhaps this is one area particularly suited to the intimacy and trust of friendship. Who can hold up convicting mirrors for us so steadily and compassionately as our dearest friends?

Another biblical image of dynamic friendship—as powerful but infinitely more poignant than that of iron sharpening iron—is that of the healing of the paralytic in Mark 2:1-12. The Gospel give us an extraordinary picture in this text (richly rewarded by meditation): Jesus is "at home" in Capernaum, preaching to such a packed house that there is no way for anyone outside even to get near the door. But so determined are the afflicted man's friends that he shall be brought to Jesus that they remove the roof of the house and lower him down on his pallet through the opening they have torn for him. "My son, your sins are forgiven" (v. 5). Clearly—marvelously—Jesus is touched by the love and faith of the paralytic's friends, who have gone to such great lengths to carry their helpless companion and lay him at Jesus' feet. This is another defining characteristic of those who are friends in Christ: When we ourselves are unable, for whatever reason, to move toward God under our own power, God grants us friends who will carry us. "A friend," quotes Aelred, "is the medicine of life. . . .

For medicine is not more powerful or efficacious for our wounds in all our temporal needs than the possession of a friend who meets every misfortune joyfully, so that, as the Apostle says, shoulder to shoulder they carry one another's burdens."[27]

Elsewhere Aelred expresses his own profound gratitude to a friend at court who apparently rescued him from calamitous self-loathing: "Terrible was the distress I felt within myself, tormenting me, corrupting my soul with intolerable stench. And *unless you had quickly stretched out your hand*, not being able to tolerate myself, I might have taken the most desperate remedy of despair."[28]

The pastoral function of friendship, stretching out our hands to each other, bearing each other's burdens, is closely related to and at least as important as the prophetic function. Both imply more intentionality and seriousness than popular notions of friendship generally assume. In fact, such an identification of functions (pastoral, prophetic) makes it clear that Christian friendship, as Aelred intended it and experienced it and celebrated it, is a kind of ministry, a ministry to which we are all called as part of our membership in the Body of Christ and for which we are all gifted.

Reclaiming Christian friendship as a real gift and call from God could have transforming potential for our life in the Church. In an immediate and practical way, fostering a vocational sense of friendship might be part of a creative solution to the felt problem of supply-and-demand mentioned at the beginning of this essay. There might not be such long waiting lists for Carmelite prioresses as spiritual directors if we were more conscious that there is a great wealth—a veritable buried treasure—of guidance, support, and nurture available to us among our own Christian friends. We might come to realize that our sudden need for a "professional" director is not so urgent as we had first thought. We might learn to see, in retrospect, that in fact all our lives, through all our crises of joy and sorrow, all our moments of discernment and choice, we have (as Lennon and McCartney remind us) gotten by with a little help from our friends.

It is a transforming moment for Jacob, after his dream of angels at Bethel, when he "awoke from sleep and said, 'Surely the LORD is in this place and I did not know it'" (Gen 28:16). Like Jacob, or like the disciples traveling together on the road to Emmaus,[29] sometimes we realize only after the fact that God has been with us. Sometimes part of that revelation of unrecognized presence is a revelation of the God-bearing friends who were present with us at the time. We see God by a creaturely light, Thomas Merton reminds us: Sometimes the luminous creatures may be angels or strangers; sometimes they are our friends.

"A faithful friend is a sturdy shelter," the Book of Wisdom affirms. "One who has found a friend has found a treasure; there is nothing as precious as a faithful friend."[30]

Recognizing the value of Christian friends to the Christian life—honoring their insights, giving thanks for their presence—does not of course require the dismantling of traditional structures of spiritual direction, with the more impersonal, unilateral, and hierarchical expectations that that relationship typically carries. Spiritual direction as it has been classically understood and practiced will no doubt continue to have a meaningful and valued place in the lives of many people, at many decisive moments in their lives. However, I do believe that claiming and honoring the role of friends in the Christian life could enormously enrich and enliven the range of possibilities for discernment and growth.

Such a sense of the worth of friendship could lead to greater depth and authenticity not only in peer relationships but in director/directee relationships as well. Without undermining the necessarily more unilateral focus of self-disclosure on the part of the directee, a deep awareness of Aelred's "we two, with Christ a third" on the part of the director would go far to foster trust and intimacy between "we two." In fact, such a closeness between people engaged in spiritual direction would mirror not only Aelred's sense of friendship but also the tenderness and depth of St. Paul's regard for the Christian community at Thessalonica: "So deeply do we care for you that we are determined to share with you not only the gospel of God but also our own selves, because you have become very dear to us" (1 Thess 2:8 NRSV).

Margaret Guenther, writing of the director's need to "know in truth" in order effectively to help with discernment of the holy in the experience of the directee, has this to say:

> To know in truth . . . is to allow oneself to be known. . . . This is the truth that became incarnate in Jesus Christ, a truth known not in abstraction but in relationship. The shared

> commitment to truth ensures that the spiritual direction relationship is one of true mutuality, for both director and directee must allow themselves to be known. This marks one of the major differences between spiritual direction and psychotherapy: the director must be willing to be known—not just by her credentials, affiliations, and titles, but known in her vulnerability and limitations as a child of God.[31]

Whether we work as spiritual directors or pastors in "professional ministry" or administer grace to each other purely in the bonds of friendship, we need each other and are privileged to love and to help each other. As St. Brigid is supposed to have said, a person without a soul friend is like a body without a head. As certain contemporary theologians remind us, the classic affirmation of God as three in one serves as an emblem of the dynamic relationship at the heart of God.

By the grace of God, we live in eternal relationship with Christ, who calls us friends and in whom we are already joined together by the mystery of baptism into the body of Christ, the Church. From that perspective it is clear that Christian friendship partakes of holy and eternal mysteries, far transcending utilitarian notions of worth. (And as Lyndall Gordon has pointed out, "To see friends as useful is, of course, to miss the whole point of friendship."[32])

Finally, then, the reclaiming of Christian friendship as part of the rich heritage of spiritual growth and support is not so much a political imperative—much less a practical solution to a staffing problem in parishes—as a recognition of a transforming reality already at work. Friendship is as much mystery as ministry.

Perhaps it is not surprising that it is a member of the Society of Friends, the American Quaker Thomas Kelly who—at least for me—most beautifully captures this sense of the sheer blessedness of the bond between friends in Christ. The chapter on "The Blessed Community" in his classic *A Testament of Devotion* is a lovely essay on the mystical grace of Christian friendship. With striking parallels to Aelred (whom he does not appear to have read, however), Kelly writes of the "Fellowship" as a gift from God: "It is a holy matrix of 'the communion of saints,' the body of Christ which is His Church. . . . The final grounds of holy fellowship are in God. Lives immersed and drowned in God are drowned in love, and know one another in Him and know one another in love."[33]

On the practical duties of friendship within the Fellowship, Kelly is as unequivocal as Aelred:

> Within the wider Fellowship emerges the special circle of a few on whom, for each of us, a particular emphasis of nearness has fallen. These are our special gift and task. These we "carry" by inward, wordless prayer. By an interior act and attitude we lift them repeatedly before the throne and hold them there in power. This is work, real labor of the soul. It takes energy but it is done in joy.[34]

Again like Aelred, Kelly can sound ultimate about the role of friendship in the Christian life. Aelred suggests that God is friendship—Kelly similarly suggests that friendship is the very fabric of the kingdom of God: "Where the Fellowship is lacking the Church invisible is lacking and the Kingdom of God has not yet come. For these bonds of divine love and 'carrying' are the stuff of the Kingdom of God. [One] who is in the Fellowship is in the Kingdom."[35]

From his own vivid experience of this aspect of the realm of God, Kelly affirms:

> Two people, three people, ten people may be in living touch with one another through Him who underlies their separate lives. . . . We know that these souls are with us, lifting their lives and ours continuously to God and opening themselves, with us, in steady and humble obedience to Him. It is as if the boundaries of our self were enlarged, as if we were within them and as if they were within us. Their strength, given to them by God, becomes our strength, and our joy, given to us by God, becomes their joy. In confidence and love we live together in Him. . . . All friendships short of this are incomplete.[36]

Perhaps if we reflect on our lives in this "creaturely light," we will come to see—with a shock of recognition and delight—that, far more than we have ever realized before, our friends in Christ have revealed God to us, have carried us in their hearts, have stretched out their hands, have held up mirrors for us that shattered dangerous illusions.

Perhaps in longing for such a friend, we may be given grace to become one, to invite the deep and joyful communion within the body of Christ that is surely part of what God intends for each of us.

For Christians, called and gifted to be friends of God and companions for each other on the way, all friendships short of this are incomplete.

— 14 —

Between Friends

We meet at noon
in a clatter of plates,
in a bright haze of chatter
and cigarette smoke.
We exchange embrace
of holy kiss and
celebrate our lives together.
The burden of our several days,
once shared, grows light
and in that light
the coffee pours out sacramental:
lunch becomes a
monumental feast of love.
And then amid the noise and clutter,
around our table angels hover.
Above the din of common things
we hear the beat
of mighty wings.

— 15 —

Angels

I SAW A BUMPER STICKER THE OTHER DAY that really bothered me: "Angels: Don't leave home without them!" The sheer inanity of it was bad enough, but it was the familiarity, the complacent assumption of entitlement to angelic convenience that was so grating—angels as a kind of heavenly American Express account: time-saving, security-enhancing, the ultimate travel accessory.

Twenty years ago, when I first began to study and lecture on the subject of angels, the whole idea was considered arcane, even bizarre. These days, though, angels are a major marketing phenomenon. Bookstores have whole sections devoted to best-selling angel books and tapes; gift stores abound with cute angel stuff, from greeting cards and candles to charms and (naturally) bumper stickers. I am afraid to check online, but I wouldn't be at all surprised to learn that angels have a home page on the Web.

This would be great news if the surge in interest in angels-as-commodity equaled interest in angels-as-divine-reality. But it doesn't. I'm afraid the present trivializing of angels is even worse than the previous decades' ignoring of them was. From not believing in angels, we have gone to believing in them in a silly, indulgent way, as if we were to pretend to take seriously our childish belief in the tooth fairy.

Now this is a shame. It impoverishes our lives—without, however, probably making much difference to the angels. As the poet Francis Thompson once observed, "The angels keep their ancient places: Turn but a stone and start a wing. Tis you, tis your estranged faces, that miss the many-splendor'd thing."

Our faces, here at the beginning of the new millennium, are

"estranged" for many different reasons. Bad theology, particularly of the puritan variety that strips all that is beautiful and imaginative from religion, can write angels out of the salvational script. Bad art that insists on portraying angels as fat naked babies with useless wings can deny the awesome power that Scripture ascribes to angelic visitation. Post-Enlightenment rationalism that demands that all human experience be empirically demonstrable leaves hardly a leg for real angels to stand on (even on the head of a pin).

But bad art and bad theology—even bad bumper stickers—by themselves wouldn't be enough to rob us of God's angels if our experience confirmed the possibility. There is an old Jewish legend that says God blinds us, in mercy, to the presence of angels because we would go mad with fear if we could see them.

That may well be so. But I suspect that sometimes angels long to be perceived and that it is not God's mercy but our myopia that keeps us blind to the angels among us.

It is worth taking the trouble to un-estrange our faces and catch a glimpse of a many-splendored thing.

Traditional Christianity, like traditional Judaism and Islam, has always affirmed the reality of angels. Important people like Thomas Aquinas and John Calvin took angels very seriously indeed. (Which is something we can be sure angels themselves never do: I think it was G. K. Chesterton who observed that "angels can fly because they take themselves so lightly.")

More importantly, of course, than even the fearfully logical witness of Aquinas and Calvin, the Bible itself is brimful of angels. And while the scriptural witness is short on physical description, it is pretty clear that, whatever they looked like, the angels that appeared to Jacob, and to Mary, and to the shepherds outside Bethlehem and Mary Magdalene outside the empty tomb were not fat naked babies with frivolous wings. It doesn't seem that there was anything remotely cute about them, since practically the first thing they ever say to anyone is "Don't be afraid." (Madeline L'Engle's description of a cherubim in *A Wind in the Door* is much more biblical than most familiar portrayals: The cherubim in that book is so awesome a creature of fire and smoke and eyes and wings that at first the children think it is a drove of dragons.)

The common denominator of the scriptural witness for angels seems to be that angels are creatures of pure spirit whose home is heaven, where they forever surround the throne of God but who are sometimes sent out on missions to the earth to manifest God's presence or announce God's plans. They are by nature essentially bodiless but sometimes assume a bodily form in order to appear to human beings.

There is strong biblical witness for guardian angels as well as messenger angels—as in Matthew 18:10, where Jesus, speaking of children, declares that "in heaven their angels always behold the face of my Father."

One of my favorite scriptural stories about guardian angels is the one in Daniel 3 about Shadrach, Meshach, and Abednego, three faithful Jews who, refusing to worship the idol established by King Nebuchadnezzar, were bound up and thrown into a fiery furnace for their treason. The blast from the open door of the furnace was so great that it killed the soldiers who threw the prisoners in. King Nebuchadnezzar watched all this, astonished, then "rose up in haste" and asked his counselors, "Did we not cast three men bound into the fire?" They answered, "True, O king." "But I see four men loose, walking in the midst of the fire, and they are not hurt; and the appearance of the fourth is like a son of the gods" (vv. 24-25).

When the king ran to open the furnace and called Shadrach, Meshach, and Abednego out, they emerged so unscathed by the fire that their clothes didn't even smell like smoke. And they emerged alone. The angel was gone, but the angel had been there when it counted, walking with them in the heart of the terrible fire.

There is also the wonderful cautionary folk tale of Balaam's ass, recorded in Numbers 22. Balaak the King of Moab asked Balaam to come and curse the Israelites; Balaam went with the king's messengers, despite God's warning that he should not go. So God became angry and sent an angel with a sword to stand in his way. Balaam's trusty donkey three times saw the angel, and three times stopped in his tracks, but Balaam (presumably because he was too preoccupied with the king's flattery) did not see the angel and beat the donkey for stopping. Then the Lord opened Balaam's eyes and Balaam saw the angel (whose first words, by the way, were to berate him for beating his donkey).

The writer of the letter to the Hebrews urges us not to "neglect to show hospitality to strangers, for thereby some have entertained angels unawares" (13:2). So the Bible suggests that our sense of our own importance can blind us to angels but that courageous witness (like that of Shadrach and company) and humility (like that of Balaam's ass), as well as hospitality to strangers, can open our eyes to the angels present with us.

According to the scriptural witness, our guardian angels promote our good, strengthen and protect us, walk with us in the fiery furnaces of our lives. Of course, since they are pure spirit, there is a limit to how much they can fight our battles for us, since our soul struggles tend to be all tangled up in physical and material nets. We must be careful not to abdicate too much responsibility to the promise of angelic aid: There are some things we must do, and refrain from doing, by ourselves.

But there is real help available to us, every moment of every day, to resist temptation, to keep our tempers, to remember our promises. When we are dying, the African-American spiritual promises us, God sends whole "bands of angels" to carry us home.

If we can teach our hearts to see, we may discover that angels are with us—not as the ultimate travel accessory, not as a kind of divine credit card, but as messengers and vehicles of grace. We may come to see them, as Balaam's donkey did, standing right in front of us, barring the way to the disaster we are intent on pursuing—or as Shadrach, Meshach, and Abednego did, walking at our sides in the midst of danger.

Even if we don't see them, we can trust their invisible presence—trust that, as the poet Richard Wilbur put it, "outside the open window, the morning air is all awash with angels."

Part 4
Fruitfulness

– 16 –

Of Woodstoves, Burnout, and the Living Flame of Love

I HAD BEEN TO THE MONASTERY many times before—in the springtime of deep mud and restless wind, in the heat of summer when the scent of dust and sun-drenched sage mingled with the incense in the chapel, in the silver nights and golden days of fall. But I had never before made a retreat "in the bleak midwinter." I thought of that Christina Rossetti poem many times that January week when "earth stood hard as iron, water like a stone."

Earth and water were immobilized, but the cold itself was like a living thing, prowling around outside my cell, waiting to pounce on me as I left the warmth of the chapel, wrapping itself around my feet in the small hours of the night. My cell was equipped with a little wood-burning stove; wood and kindling were neatly stacked in a corner; user-friendly instructions were posted on the wall. I was blithely dismissive when the guestmaster offered to explain the idiosyncrasies of my little stove. Surely any fool could light a fire and keep it burning; how tricky could it be?

Challenges of Fire Tending

Well, I have eaten tastier words. My airy nonchalance was to leave a distinctly smoky taste in my mouth before the retreat was over. I was to become intimately acquainted with my own arrogance, ignorance, and helplessness over the next few days—as well as with the stubborn mysteries of grates, dampers, drafts, and flues.

The first morning, I awakened to freezing cold and leaped from my bed to discover only cold ashes in a blackened grate. The cheerful blaze I had triumphantly accomplished at bedtime the night before had gone completely out—through my own fault by what I had done (left the vent open too far) and what I had failed to do (put on more wood when I got up for Lauds).

With stiff fingers that kept fumbling the matches and dropping the kindling, I managed to start the fire again (realizing ruefully only afterward that not one word of the charming and ancient Celtic blessing for "Lighting a New Fire" had occurred to me).

After Mass I checked my stove anxiously. It still burned, by the grace of God, but barely. (It was then I first noticed the word "Intrepid" emblazoned on the iron doors.) I was about to pile more wood on the struggling fire to ensure steady heat for my morning *lectio* when all at once I remembered the advice of St. Teresa of Avila, read many years ago. Teresa warned that we must be careful not to extinguish a small fire with heavy logs: "A little straw put there with humility . . . will serve the purpose and help more to enkindle the fire than a lot of wood. . . . These, in our opinion, would smother the spark within the space of a Creed."[1]

Of course, St. Teresa was speaking metaphorically of the need for a light touch in prayer. Nevertheless, I suspect that this most delightfully down-to-earth of mystics would be amused to know that she had given such practical assistance for a cross and chilly monastery guest. I promptly followed her advice, substituting twentieth-century newspaper for the sixteenth-century straw, and soon had (for a while at any rate) a good blaze going.

Keeping that fire burning was to become a central preoccupation of my retreat. I learned by trial and error how to give it the frequent and careful attention it required—remembering to put on a log before going to Vespers to keep it going until Compline, at bedtime remembering to close the damper a bit, putting fuel at the ready for when I awoke in the night, shaking down the ashes in the morning.

My second night at the monastery, as I left my warm blankets to feed the fire, coaxing the sleepy flames to take the nourishment of split pine, I was powerfully reminded of the days (and nights) when my daughters were babies. Not since that time of early motherhood had I awakened in the dark for a two o'clock feeding. The mindful, disciplined, constant care of winter fire began to emerge as a sustaining metaphor not only for my retreat but also for a life of Christian faith and ministry.

The Flame of Love

Perhaps it is not surprising—since the canon was established and most of the saints in the calendar lived a considerable time before central heating was invented—that the image of fire is such a dominant one in classical writings about the spiritual life. The prophet Isaiah reminds us that God deals tenderly with the weak by declaring that "a dimly burning wick he will not quench" (Isa 42:3). Paul's advice to Timothy includes the admonition to "rekindle the gift of God that is within you . . . ; for God did not give us a spirit of timidity but a spirit of power and love and self-control" (2 Tim 1:6). Perhaps the most famous use of fire as an image of the spiritual life is in the work of the great Spanish mystic and poet, St. John of the Cross. His poem *Llama De Amor Viva* celebrates the divine fire, the "living flame of love" that tenderly wounds the soul.[2]

Much of the concern about fires over the centuries has been just to keep them burning. (It was a great comfort to me to realize this: I was not alone in my struggle.) It also intrigued me that the current name for spiritual exhaustion is "burnout." Obviously the whole idea of inner light and fire goes very deep. We seem to know that we must have this fire to live, and that it is at risk.

All of us as Christians—especially as ministers, teachers, parents, pastors, and directors—have a special responsibility to cherish and to tend what St. John called the "living flame of love," a flame that God has kindled within those persons entrusted to our care and within ourselves.

What can we do when the fire grows cold?

The implications for ministry are pretty clear. We are called to tend "the living flame of love." We must become intimately acquainted with the special qualities of each fire within our care, so that we will know best how to respond—when to add more fuel, when to leave well enough alone, when a prodding is all that is required, when (as St. Teresa notes) it would be wise to "blow a little with our intellects."[3]

The implications are perhaps less clear but no less significant for the self-care of those in ministry. As physicians are notoriously careless of their own health, so those most engaged in religious life are often least attentive to the state of their own souls. Many of us are in the midst of winter in our own lives, burdened with fatigue and disappointment and sorrow. Like Dante, we may find ourselves "in the middle of a dark wood."

How are we tending our own inner fires?

We will all, from time to time, become aware that we are "burning dimly." The zeal that first informed our apostolates has faded; God who once seemed so close is distant; prayer that nourished us is now arid, empty. The fire in our hearts that once was kindled (at birth, at baptism, at ordination) and that once blazed hot and clear has somehow fallen into smoldering embers. How then do we respond?

There is sometimes a temptation, in my own experience and observation of dying fire, to shrug and let the tiresome thing go out. We may feel this temptation as a kind of irritable weariness. (At the monastery, at two in the morning, I awoke to warning cold but only burrowed under the blankets, muttering crossly, "So go ahead and die; only let me sleep.") To the extent that we in our pastoral work function as social workers, therapists, or community organizers, it may sometimes (secretly, of course) occur to us that the religious-vocation aspect of our professional lives is just a nuisance, just another nagging demand. Think of all the time we would save, these demons whisper, if we didn't always have to be getting up early for morning *lectio*, or going to church, or examining conscience. We might be colder, yes, but wouldn't we be more efficient, less distracted from the "real" work that crowds on us so urgently?

Or perhaps, with similar impatience and equally disastrous results, we lose our tempers and pile on heavy logs in the form of punishing overwork or severe penances or whatever. This way, of course, the fire is quenched as thoroughly as and even more quickly than if we had done nothing at all.

Alternatively, we may panic upon finding only cold ashes in a blackened grate and abandon our other duties in order to concentrate all our energies on relighting the fire of vocation or faith.

St. Teresa's Insights

None of these responses, variously reflecting the deadly sins of acedia, anger, and pride, will do much to keep the home fires burning. On the contrary, great patience, humility, and trust are called for.

Also, as usual in the deepest struggles of the spiritual life, a sense of humor will help enormously—and thanks be to God for companions on the way. St. Teresa is an especially valuable fellow pilgrim and fire watcher, I began to realize, both as I browsed in the monastery library and as I knelt in my cell before my recalcitrant stove. Her words in *The Book of Her Life* are particularly apropos:

> But even though the soul puts wood on the fire and does this little it can do of itself, the fire of love does not burn. It is through His great mercy that it sees at least the smoke so as to know that the fire is not entirely dead. The Lord returns to rekindle it. For even though a soul breaks its head in arranging the wood and blowing on the fire, it seems that everything it does only smothers the fire more.[4]

Fussing, in other words, is not much good, nor frenzied "arranging the wood and blowing on the fire"—trying by main force to keep enthusiasm high, whether by racing from one book or conference or director to another, or by implementing more and more programs in a parish in which interest seems to be waning. How often have we all done that? And how often have we seen our efforts only put out the fire more and more?

Justification is by grace alone, Martin Luther declared. The fire of divine love, Teresa similarly reminds us, proceeds from God alone: "For however much I may desire and seek and strive after it, I play no part in obtaining even a spark of it, save when His Majesty so desires, as I have often said."[5]

As is so often the case (and as of course St. John of the Cross so ably reminds us), we must sometimes wait through the dark night for the living flame to appear. The place to begin is in cold and prayerful waiting, learning by experience, as Teresa remarks, how little we can do on our own, and trusting that somehow God "will return and kindle" the fire in our hearts.

This is where trust is essential. Our fear and despair themselves can quench the last glowing coals. Teresa comments: "It is truly a great suffering. Since the soul lacks the strength to throw some wood on this fire and is dying lest the fire go out, I think that within itself it is being consumed and turned to ashes and dissolved in tears and burnt up."[6]

This is a perilous moment for the soul but also an opportunity for great grace. Teresa goes on to say that at this point, "dying" and "dissolved in tears," we ought in fact to be most grateful to God: "Let the soul who has reached this state praise the Lord. . . . For such a soul doesn't know or understand the blessing it has unless it has experienced a taste of what it is to be unable to do anything in the service of the Lord, and yet always receive a great deal."[7]

Deep and prolonged life in God will probably mean starting over, time after time, realizing over and over again that apart from God we can do nothing. (On my retreat, I used a mortifyingly huge number of matches, lighting and relighting fires that had gone out. Thanks be to God for Ohio Bluetip.)

Paradoxically, when God has rekindled the flame of love again, we hold our abandonment to divine providence in tension with our own responsibility. Listen to St. Teresa again:

> This love also seems like a huge fire that always needs something to burn so as not to go out. Thus in the case of the souls I'm speaking of, even were it to cost them a great deal, they would want to carry wood so that this fire might not be extinguished. I am the kind who is made happy even with pieces of straw I can throw on it; and this I do sometimes—or many times.[8]

We must do all we can; we must "carry wood so that this fire might not be extinguished." If it does go out despite our best efforts, we must pray and wait for God to kindle it again—completely abandoned to the divine will but alert for the tiniest spark to feed with straw. Quiet watchfulness seems to be key—not frantically rearranging the wood or piling on heavy logs. Certainly abandoning the hearth is not an option. God does not give up on us, and we are not allowed to give up on ourselves. Neither are we encouraged to weep over the ashes. The difficulty in acknowledging that we must care for ourselves when we are tired or weak is that we so quickly succumb to the delicious temptation of self-pity.

Self-Care

It is abundantly clear from St. Teresa's use of the metaphor of divine fire that we are charged by God to nurture carefully what has been entrusted to us. We are not invited to indulge ourselves, make excuses, or be permanently satisfied with less than God intends for us. Ordinary common sense and good stewardship require that we not permit the loss to God of what has been left in our care for the light of the world.

A discipline of straw will keep us gentle with ourselves but not permissive. The point is to keep the flame burning, not to keep it small. St. Teresa suggests that sometimes we simply need to relinquish our illusion of control. When the soul is driving itself crazy blowing on the fire and rearranging the wood, Teresa declares: "I believe the best thing for it to do is to surrender itself completely to the fact that of itself it can do nothing and to become occupied, as I said, in some other meritorious works. For perhaps the Lord removes the prayer so that it might undertake these works and come to know through experience how little it can do by itself."[9]

One of the perils to be avoided, apparently, is the temptation to become self-absorbed to the neglect of clear duties, as well as the temptation simply to give up. The "calm strength and patient wisdom"[10] that fire tending demands will enable us to endure the hardships of the long haul; they are not meant to get us off the hook.

One of the stalwart "Desert Mothers," Amma Syncletica, reflected centuries ago that "in the beginning, there are a great many battles and a good deal of suffering for those who are advancing to God, and afterwards, ineffable joy. It is like those who wish to light a fire; at first they are choked by the smoke and cry. . . . So we also must kindle the divine fire in ourselves through prayer and hard work."[11]

Smoke gets in our eyes. We weep and struggle. We learn. We become able to discern what will keep the dimly burning fire from going out: when we need a light touch, when we need to depend afresh on God, when we need to ask for help, when we need just to keep on keeping on.

We can do much for ourselves and for each other in these disciplines of straw. Rest and healthy food, sensible exercise, unpressured prayer—knowing when "great logs of wood" would extinguish the uncertain flame—may sometimes be just what the Lord requires of us. When one of her daughters was sick or discouraged, St. Teresa would sometimes take her supper on a tray, not demand (or permit) penitential mortifications that might quench the smoking fire. Evelyn Underhill, another shrewd and loving director, similarly prescribed bed rest and Jane Austen novels for an overwrought friend who, in shame for her "weakness," was attempting fasts and vigils instead.

I suspect that our failure to take care of ourselves in these moments as we would naturally care for others is not so much because we do not know what we need as because we refuse to admit that we need anything at all. Sometimes, as Simone Weil once pointed out, we are in danger of starving to death not because there is no bread but because we insist that we are not hungry.[12]

Those who have learned to be patient with themselves in times of exhaustion know (ironically) what self-control and discipline these moments require—when in our despair we may long only for the finality of extinction, or in our impatience with our weakness are tempted to go out in a final blaze of glory. These same people often experience what St. John of the Cross called "*O mano blando, o toque delicado*" ("the gentle hand, the delicate touch") of God in their quiet waiting.[13] This surrender to God, this acknowledgment of helplessness, requires much courage—but amazing grace abounds.

This "living flame of love" belongs to God, as do we. God wills the fire to blaze in us. By the grace of God, we are entrusted with the care of fire, that the flame "once shadowy and blind" may "flare in the light and warmth and wake the love with amazing joy."[14]

Conclusion

By the end of my retreat, I had learned a great deal from that stove named "Intrepid." I made many mistakes; I learned from most of them. When I succeeded, on my last night at the monastery, in lighting the fire without filling the room with choking smoke and in keeping it burning throughout the small hours, I was filled with gratitude, relief, and joy (to say nothing of warmth and light). Surely God is pleased when we manage in our inner lives, as well, not to quench the dimly burning "flame of love."

God grant us patience and humility to feed the inner fire with straw when it subsides. For as St. Teresa exclaimed, "O my Jesus, how much a soul can do when ablaze with your love!"[15]

– 17 –

Sparks Among the Stubble

You Can Catch Fire

ONCE UPON A TIME, the ancient story goes, one hermit in the desert sought the counsel of another. The young monk came to the older one and said, "Abba, according as I am able, I keep my little rule, and my little fast, my prayer, meditation and contemplative silence; and according as I am able, I strive to cleanse the thoughts of my heart; now what more should I do?" The elder rose up in reply and stretched out his hands to heaven, and his fingers became like ten torches of flame. He asked, "Why not be totally changed into fire?"

We can be, you know. We can catch fire, shine like beacons, blaze like torches in the night for the glory of God, for the transforming of the world.

Fire is elemental, archetypal in human experience. For thousands of years it has been an important sign for the people of God. A sign of presence, like the pillar of fire that accompanied the Israelites into the desert nights of the exodus, like the burning bush from which God spoke to Moses. Fire is a sign of judgment, of passion, of transforming and purifying power.

Fire is also a sign of the reign of Christ. "I baptize you with water," John the Baptist told the people who sought him out on the banks of the Jordan River. "But he who is coming after me . . . will baptize you with the Holy Spirit *and with fire*" (Matt 3:11, emphasis added). On the day of Pentecost, grace like tongues of fire descended from heaven, pure gift to all who were gathered there. That fire has never been extinguished. It is spreading still.

We can catch fire.

In the Gospel of Luke, Jesus—himself aflame with conviction

and longing—exclaims, "I came to cast fire upon the earth, and how I wish it were already kindled!" (Luke 12:49 NRSV). The gnostic gospel of Thomas echoes that dramatic firelit image of the One who is the light of the world: "Whoever is near to me," Jesus promises, "is near to the fire. Whoever is far from me is far from the Kingdom."[1]

Winter's Fire

I grew up in a small town in Kansas, right on the edge of the wheat fields—not, one would expect, a world of apocalyptic signs, of pillars of fire and smoke. But, for a few weeks every winter, it was.

In the bleak midwinter, every year, sometime in February I think, the farmers in Harvey County would burn off the old stubble in their fields to get them ready for the spring planting. For all I know, they do it still—but for me that childhood memory has the mythic, dreamlike feel of ancient mystery. I have never forgotten the sight: the watchful farmers leaning on their rakes. The slow creeping of the low flames. The leaping showers of sparks. The veils of acrid smoke. The black, exhausted-looking patches left behind. Burnt, dead stubble through which, in a few weeks, the green blades of the new wheat would begin to rise.

The annual ritual of the burning of the fields has stayed with me all these years as a powerful image of the dynamic, transforming mystery of fire.

We can catch fire.

Sometimes, in our chilled weariness with this broken world, we draw near to the fire of Christ intending only to warm our own cold hands and hearts. But as we draw close, we will be not only comforted but ignited. That is the marvelous, dangerous opportunity at the heart of our faith.

We can catch fire.

We can run like sparks through the stubble.

The apocryphal book of the Wisdom of Solomon assures us that we shall. The souls of the blessed, it says, "will shine forth, and will run like sparks through the stubble."[2] We can burn with the renewing holy fire of God. Not just for our own sakes, but for the sake of the world, for the sake of all people who sit in darkness and in cold.

Stubble on Fire

There is, I imagine, in each of our lives a considerable acreage of stubble. Fields that once were green with hope, ripe with promise, lie blighted or barren. Sorrow, death, betrayal, disappointment; broken dreams in public and in private life, in our families, our work, our churches. The cumulative effect of inner and outer loss can leave us feeling that we live permanently in rural February, surrounded by blunt, stubbled fields as far as the eye can see.

It is easier sometimes to see the traces of past harvests than the green blades rising.

Nevertheless, we can catch fire. We can run like sparks through the stubble.

We will join a long and ardent tradition if we do so. From the very beginning, people touched by Jesus have been people touched by flame. Long before the desert fathers and mothers, Jesus' first disciples and friends caught fire, and ran with it into the world, torch-bearers for the light that shines in darkness. The New Testament burns with the glow of these ignited lives.

The Gospel accounts of the women around Jesus are, for instance, stories of women on fire. Women Jesus knew and called by name—women Jesus loved and set free. Women so changed by Jesus' love for them that they were able to draw near to him and stay beside him when everyone else had fled.

They had received his healing, claiming touch on their bodies and their minds; they had stood at the foot of the cross. They were the first witnesses to the resurrection, the first to proclaim the good news. The women were the very first to share the faith, to run like sparks through the stubble.

Of course, we can only spread the fire with which we burn; we can only share the faith we have.

Fire of Our Lives

So it is vitally important that we ask ourselves: What do we really trust? Whom do we truly seek? What is the central truth of our lives that we are burning to tell?

As good Christians, some of us raised on the Heidelburg Catechism, we know the "right" answer to that—in God alone are we meant to trust. The Brief Statement of Faith reminds us (in its first and perhaps only noncontroversial line), "In life and in death we belong to God."[3] We were created for nothing else than to live and die and live forever, trusting only in God, relying only on the glorious promise that nothing can separate us from the love of God.

But in fact we rely on a lot of other things as well. We have enormous faith in our own past, for instance, and in our future, and in our institutions, in our church. And that may be very right and proper, very natural. But that is exactly where we must be very careful.

Because our past cannot save us. Neither can our future, nor the church, nor the *Book of Order*, nor doing all things decently and in order. Only God can save us, the God who creates us and calls us and loves us into being and will never leave us. As an old Scottish hymn reminds us, "On Christ the solid rock we stand—all other ground is sinking sand."[4]

The faith that is in us is the only faith we can share. The fire that burns in us is the only fire we can spread.

How then do we become totally turned into flame? How can we run like sparks through the stubble?

All we have to do is draw near to God, near enough to catch fire. Near enough to want nothing more than that.

Like Mary Magdalene, we can receive the healing, claiming touch of Christ. We can salute with joy and gratitude the love at the heart of the universe that calls us by name and sets us free and sends us out to kindle fire on the earth.

Being totally changed into fire is neither complicated nor difficult. It is not a problem to be solved but a mystery to be lived and celebrated. If we wish, God's fire can happen to us. If we want it, it *will* happen to us. Perhaps God will open our eyes and we will see that it *has* happened to us.

If we get close enough to the fiery heart of God, the white-hot refining fire at the center of the vortex, we will catch fire ourselves. We will not have to worry about how to share it with others. As a friend of mine once pointed out to a gathering of people fretting about the ways and means of evangelism, if you are in love, you cannot hide it. If you are pregnant, it will show.

If we are on fire with the passionate love of God, if something marvelous is at work within us, changing us and reshaping us, eager to use us as agents of the new creation, the grandeur of God will show. "It will flame out, like shining from shook foil."[5] It will pour out of us like water, like wine, like light from mirrors dazzled by the sun.

We will run like Mary to proclaim the good news. We will run like sparks through the stubble. Burning off the old, preparing the fields for new life, the life for which we were created, the life that will never die.

— 18 —

Vine and Branches

Abiding in Christ

MANY YEARS AGO, when our children were small, we spent a family holiday in northern Italy. One of the (many) things that rejoiced my heart about that rugged landscape was how biblical it seemed: Silvery groves of fig and olive trees crowned the hills, the steeply terraced slopes were planted row on row with vines.

The only grapevine I had ever seen before was the one in my great-grandmother's Ohio garden—a graceful Concord specimen, prized for the jewel-like jelly made every fall from its fruit. But that single cherished plant had not prepared me for the sight of Tuscan vineyards, mile upon leafy mile of vine and branches, trained to regimental order along wooden fences to make the most of the life-giving sun and rain.

We rented an old farmhouse for our holiday that week; walking into the nearby town of Barga every day gave me abundant opportunities for a closer look at those vines. Some of them were young and fragile looking, with translucent leaves and tiny stem-like branches; others were massive, gnarled, and obviously ancient. It was difficult to see where one of the old vines began and another ended, almost impossible to trace back with my eyes the myriad tangled branches, twined over and extending far down their supporting railings to the vital root in the ground.

But of course, visible or not, that connection was essential: If at any point, any one of those abundant vines were to be cut off from the root and the elaborate system of long-distance transportation of nutrients were to be severed, the branches would quickly wither and perish, the small green fruit never ripen for harvest.

And so it is with us. In one of the most powerful and evocative images in the Gospels, Jesus tells his disciples, "I am the vine, you are the branches. Those who abide in me and I in them bear much fruit, because apart from me you can do nothing" (John 15:5 NRSV).

For early Christians, Mediterranean people keenly aware of the importance of grapes and wine for family life and community celebration, this image would have had a particularly pungent relevance. And even for those of us for whom vineyards may be only metaphors, the image of vine and branches is redolent of the fruitfulness of our life in Christ—our calling to "bear much fruit," to "produce good works" in the world.

This analogy of vine and branches has long been at the heart of my own understanding of Christian community, Eucharistic mystery, and vocation. When I was a child, the minister of our Presbyterian church repeated a portion of that vine-and-branches passage from John's Gospel every time he distributed the bread and cup to the serving elders as we observed the sacrament of the Lord's Supper. I grew up in the church with those words echoing inside me: worship inextricably entwined with work, closeness to God identified with fruitfulness.

Therein precisely lies the richness of the image—and the danger. The focus within much liberal Protestant life has typically been on "producing much fruit" rather than "abiding in Christ." We seem to appropriate readily the aspect of Jesus' metaphor that best affirms our own core values—productivity and effectiveness—while ignoring the contemplative element of "abiding" in God. We tend to be preoccupied with the urgent needs of the world that require us to "bear much fruit."

There is a perilous tendency in Christian activism to cut ourselves off from the vine. In our passion for justice, in our impatience for change, what we may fear most is being able to "do nothing." Believing that faith without works is dead (Jas 2:17), we can come to believe that social change is more urgent than (and can without cost be severed from) contemplative contact with the source of all life. We may persuade ourselves, as Henri Nouwen confesses he did for years, that being "relevant, popular, and powerful" are necessary "ingredients of effective ministry"—when in truth "these are not vocations but temptations."[1]

Cutting ourselves off from the life-giving vine in our lives as Christians has at least two dangers: First, we will probably become engrossed in the visible results of our doing" (forgetting Henri Nouwen's warning that in order to be "real agents of change [we] have to be contemplatives at heart");[2] second, we may never develop much stamina for seasons of drought and failure. Either way, we risk losing the radical unity with Christ the Vine that he intends for us.

We risk forgetting that even more deeply and essentially, the image of vine and branches speaks to the necessity of making ourselves available to the hidden depths of God—even if in fact there is no harvest. If we identify the life-giving goodness and sovereignty of God too closely with the fruitfulness of our own lives, we will be tempted to feel abandoned by God or to assume that God is neither good nor sovereign when calamity occurs.

The prophet Habakkuk, writing about 600 B.C.E., during the worst of the Babylonian captivity, braved the question of why God seems to countenance the treacherous and is "silent when the wicked swallow those more righteous than they" (Hab 1:13 NRSV). The answer he received assured him that God is eternally present and sovereign: "There is still a vision for the appointed time. . . . If it seems to tarry, wait for it; it will surely come" (Hab 2:3 NRSV). The book ends with a song of luminous serenity and trust in the face of utter desolation:

> Though the fig tree does not blossom,
> and no fruit is on the vines,
> though the produce of the olive fails
> and the fields yield no food;
> though the flock is cut off from the fold
> and there is no herd in the stalls,
> yet I will rejoice in the LORD,
> I will exult in the God of my salvation.
> (Hab 3:17-18 NRSV)

Not only the agricultural reality of vineyards but also their symbolic religious value would have been apparent to Jesus' disciples: Throughout the Hebrew scriptures Israel is identified as a vineyard planted and tended by God (e.g., Ps 80:8-15; Jer 2:21; Ezek 15:1-8). The very familiarity of the image, though, may have made it difficult for Jesus' hearers (as it is for us, for different reasons) to understand what a radical departure his own use of the metaphor represented.

In Jesus' analogy of the vine, the "true vine" is not Israel or the Church (a people in God, a community charged to bear much fruit); Jesus himself is the vine. It is his life, his love, his communion with the Father, the shedding of his blood (the fruit of the vine) that creates the possibility of the true people of God. We are members of the body of Christ not because of our ancestry or our own good works but simply because we abide in him, absolutely dependent on the life he offers. The significance of this difference is huge. It means not only that no fruitful life is possible apart from such abiding; it means that such abiding in Christ, radically available to the life he longs to pour into us, will bear fruit we could never, by ourselves, produce—or even imagine.

The heart of our vocation as Christians is not achieving ambitious goals of our own devising. Our vocation is simply to stay so indissolubly attached to Jesus, the true vine, "that Christ may dwell in [our] hearts" (Eph 3:17). The essence of our call is a mystical union with Christ so deep that we, "being rooted and grounded in love, may have power . . . to know the love of Christ which surpasses knowledge," that we "may be filled with all the fullness of God" (Eph 3:17-19).

Far from leading us into a kind of passive quietism that is absorbed in its own mystical consolations and unconcerned with the needs of the world, however, really surrendering to the "fullness" of God will inexorably draw us deeper into a passionate, self-giving love for the world God loves.

The lives of the saints are full of examples of this kind of abiding, a deep union with Christ that yields a rich harvest of radiant confidence in the love of God. The mystics seem to live securely within the peace that passes understanding, finding—and transmitting—an established peace in the midst of desolation.

Edith Stein, who became Sister Teresa Benedicta of the Cross, knew this peace. She was a brilliant young Jewish philosopher who converted to Christianity in 1922. Studying the work of Thomas Aquinas led her to see that "the deeper one is drawn into God, the more [one] needs to go out of [oneself]—out into the world, that is, to carry the divine life into it."[3] True to this vision of a holy life, for years she not only lived a demanding life of prayer and academic work but also spent many unobtrusive hours among the poor of the city.

Carrying within her this balanced awareness of contemplation and action, of abiding and bearing fruit, she entered an enclosed order of Carmelite nuns in 1933. Rather than thus seeking to escape the fate of the Jewish people, however, she clearly saw her contemplative vocation and her surrender to the will of God in all circumstances as a means of participating in the suffering of the Jews, as well as a mystical cooperation in the redemptive love of Jesus.

When the Gestapo arrested her at her convent in Holland in 1942, she was ready. At Westerbork, the central detention camp in north Holland where the prisoners awaited transport to Auschwitz, the peace that radiated from her, survivors say, was conspicuous. Several have testified to her "complete calm" as she and the other women tended the frightened children, "comforting, helping, and consoling them."[4]

One Dutch official at Westerbork recalled a conversation with Edith Stein during her stay "in that hellhole" in which she observed that, despite the terrible oppositions now operative in the world, "in the end . . . there will only be the fullness of love. How could it be otherwise?"[5]

This crucial distinction between world-defined fruitfulness (power, success, relevance) and Christ-centered fruitfulness (a life deeply rooted in God's love) was one that Henri Nouwen felt more and more keenly toward the end of his life. "The question is not: How many people take you seriously? How much are you going to accomplish? Can you show some results? But: Are you in love with Jesus?"[6]

Nouwen found himself grappling with these questions in his own life when he left his prestigious faculty position at Harvard Divinity School to work with profoundly handicapped people at the L'Arche community in Toronto. It was a disorienting, eventually transformative transition for him: to live among people who neither knew nor cared that the man feeding and dressing them was a famous professor and writer, an internationally sought-after "expert" on Christian spirituality.

That transition made him reexamine his assumptions about vocation and fruitfulness. "To live a life that is not dominated by the desire to be relevant but is instead safely anchored in the knowledge of God's first love, we have to be mystics," Nouwen declared. "Christian leaders cannot simply be persons who have well-formed opinions about the burning issues of our time. Their leadership must be rooted in the permanent, intimate relationship with the Incarnate Word, Jesus. . . . For Christian leadership to be truly fruitful, a movement from the moral to the mystical is required."[7]

In most places in the world where grapes are grown, the precious fruit must be protected from the predations of birds and rodents (and humans). Like shepherds who watch the flocks, watchers keep vigil over vines ripe for harvest. In the Tuscan vineyards past which I walked that long-ago spring, the remains of autumn's watchers' sheds could still be seen: rudimentary shelters left, temporarily abandoned, among the vines.

The German poet Rilke wrote a poem, "Just as the watchman in the wine fields," that is brimful of serene trust, saturated with contemplative silence.[8] As the watcher in the wine fields keeps awake through the long nights, so Rilke imagines himself to be a shed held in God's arms. The tone of the poem is quiet, the shape of it a prayer: direct address to a present but unseen God.

The nocturnal peace in the vineyard of the poem, like the peace within the watcher himself, is palpable. Completely self-abandoned to the Vintner, the watcher feels no anxiety for the harvest entrusted to his care; he seems to know that all he has been asked to do is stay awake, only remain present as the shed in God's arms. Neither is God anxious about the harvest or the watcher's vigilance; God does not ask if he is keeping watch or not: "Confident, dissolved by the juices, your depths keep climbing past me silently."

In the companionable silence of close friends, or of lovers, the watcher and God in Rilke's poem keep intimate company with each other and participate together in a miracle of transformation: The very depths of God, dissolved by the juices of the fruit, ascend silently in the night toward their own purposes.

For us as for Rilke's watcher, the "depths" of God begin and end where we cannot see or follow, and may lead us where we would not have thought of going. Nonetheless, we are rooted and grounded in that mystery, which is the sap in our leaves and branches, the Eucharistic wine in our mouths, the blood in our veins, "the force" (as the poet Dylan Thomas put it) "that through the green fuse drives the flower."[9]

We, like the watcher in the wine fields, can come to know profoundly that our "work" is only to remain present and aware, grateful to be held in God's arms, "rooted and grounded in love." We too can trust God to be present and active, to take care of the harvest. Then God's "depths will climb past us steadily" and carry us with them, "dissolved by the juices." If we are that securely rooted in Christ, nothing can separate us from the vine; and that is all that matters. Then we will be "safely anchored in the knowledge of God's first love"; we will be "truly fruitful"; we will, in fact, as Nouwen assures us, "be mystics."

As in those venerable Tuscan vineyards, we living branches will be so inextricably bound with the vine that it will be impossible to tell where Christ ends and we begin: one life, one purpose, one harvest.

Then, even "though the fig tree does not blossom, and no fruit is on the vines"—even though our dreams fall in ashes and all our best efforts come to naught—we too can rejoice in the Lord and exult in the God of our salvation.

– 19 –

Ash Wednesday

Heads bent.
Minds' wings folded.
The room is filled with prayer.
Murmured hope and adoration,
whispered penitence is there.
Rising wind of common sigh
held aloft, suspended high
in transcendent, burdened air:
breath of smoke from holy fire.
Then petition's warm wind lifts it,
and to Heaven sends it, gives it,
ascending
from the bent heads,
bent for God.

Notes

Introduction

1. C. S. Lewis, *Letters to Malcolm, Chiefly on Prayer* (London: Geoffrey Bles, 1964), 120.
2. C. S. Lewis, *Letters to Malcolm,* 100-101.
3. Thomas Merton, *The Seven Storey Mountain* (Garden City, N.Y.: Doubleday, 1973), 233.
4. Gerard Manley Hopkins, "God's Grandeur," in *The Poems of Gerard Manley Hopkins* (London: Oxford University Press, 1984), 66.
5. Teilhard de Chardin, *The Divine Milieu* (New York: Harper & Row, 1968), 132.
6. Evelyn Underhill, *Practical Mysticism* (London: J. M. Dent & Sons, 1914; repr., Columbus, Ohio: Ariel Press, 1986), 186.
7. See also Evelyn Underhill, *The Spiritual Life* (London: Hodder & Stoughton, 1937; repr., Harrisburg, Pa.: Morehouse, 1996), 58-59, quoting the French seventeenth-century Cardinal de Berullé's categories of "Adoration, Adherence, and Cooperation."
8. C.S. Lewis, *Prince Caspian* (New York: Macmillan, 1951), 82.
9. Robert Frost, "The Figure a Poem Makes," in *Collected Poems of Robert Frost* (New York: Henry Holt & Co., 1939), ii.

Chapter 4: To See with the Eyes of the Heart

1. G. B. Shaw, *Saint Joan: A Chronicle Play in Six Scenes* (Baltimore:

Penguin, 1968), scene 1, 59.

2. C. S. Lewis, "Sometimes Fairy Stories May Say Best What's to Be Said," in *Of This and Other Worlds* (ed. Walter Hooper; London: Collins, 1982), 73.
3. Thomas Aquinas, *Summa Theologica,* "Treatise on Angels," pt. 1, quoted by Mortimer Adler, *The Angels and Us* (New York: Macmillan, 1982), 75.
4. Wim Wenders, interview by David Sterritt, *Christian Science Monitor,* 16 December 1993: p. 15, col. 3.
5. C. S. Lewis, *George MacDonald: An Anthology* (New York: Macmillan, 1948), 20.
6. C. S. Lewis, *The Voyage of the Dawn Treader* (New York: Macmillan, 1952), 71.
7. Elizabeth Barrett Browning, "Aurora Leigh," in *Elizabeth Barrett Browning: Selected Poems* (New York: Random House, 1995).
8. Avery Brooke, *Hidden in Plain Sight: The Practice of Christian Meditation* (Nashville: Upper Room Books, 1986), 10.
9. Shaw, *Saint Joan,* scene 5, 106.
10. C.S. Lewis, *George MacDonald: An Anthology*, p. 21.

Chapter 6: The Examen Reexamined

1. At St. Beuno's College in North Wales. I am deeply grateful to Father Paul Edwards, S.J., for his wise direction.
2. George A. Aschenbrenner, "Consciousness Examen," *Review for Religious*, vol. 31, 1972/I: 14-21.
3. "A Method for Making the General Examination of Conscience," in *The Spiritual Exercises of Saint Ignatius* (trans. and commentary George E. Ganss, S. J.; St. Louis: Institute of Jesuit Sources, 1992), 38 (Sp. Ex. 43).
4. Wim Wenders, interview by David Sterritt, Christian Science Monitor, 16 December 1993: p. 15, col. 3.
5. From "Collect for Purity," in The Book of Common Prayer (New York: Church Hymnal Corporation and Seabury Press, 1979), 355.
6. The Book of Common Prayer, 361.
7. Aschenbrenner, "Consciousness Examen," 18 (emphasis added).
8. Father Dermot Preston, S.J., in a booklet on the Examen prepared for use at Loyola Hall, Merseyside, U.K.

9. Elizabeth Jennings, "Prayer Yet Could Be a Dance," in *Praying with the English Poets* (comp. and intro. Ruth Etchells; London: Triangle Books, 1990), 45.
10. Thomas Keating, *Open Mind, Open Heart: The Contemplative Dimension of the Gospel* (Rockport, Mass.: Element Books, 1986), 110.

Chapter 9: Broken Pieces

1. Post communion prayer, Holy Eucharist II, The Book of Common Prayer (New York: Church Hymnal Corporation, 1979), 365.

Chapter 10: Do You Want to Be Healed?

1. Emily Dickinson, no. 1099 in *Final Harvest: Emily Dickinson's Poems* (comp. and intro. Thomas H. Johnson; Boston: Little Brown & Co., 1961), 245.
2. Literally "the Jews," i.e., the strict Pharisees who opposed Jesus. See the exegetical commentary by Wilbert F. Howard, *The Gospel According to Luke and John,* vol. 8 of *The Interpreter's Bible* (ed. George Arthur Buttrick; New York: Abingdon Press, 1952), 542.
3. Raymond E. Brown, *The Gospel According to John I–XII,* vol. 29 of *The Anchor Bible* (Garden City, N.Y.: Doubleday, 1966), 209.
4. Simone Weil, *Waiting for God* (trans. Emma Craufurd; New York: Harper Colophon, 1973), 210.

Chapter 11: Wounded and Healed

1. "The Prayers of the People, Form VI," in The Book of Common Prayer (New York: Church Hymnal Corp., 1979), 392.
2. Michael Mayne, former dean of Westminster Abbey, describing an abbey service for the centenary of the British Deaf Association, which was translated for the profoundly deaf congregation into sign language in *Pray, Love, Remember* (London: Darton, Longman & Todd, 1998), 36.
3. Psalm 80:5, The Book of Common Prayer, 702.
4. J. R. R. Tolkein, *The Return of the King* (Boston: Houghton Mifflin, 1967), 310.
5. C. S. Lewis, *A Grief Observed* (London: Faber & Faber, 1961), 43.
6. Ibid., 24.

7. Ibid., 50-51.
8. Mayne, *Pray, Love, Remember,* 50.
9. Viktor Frankl, *Man's Search for Meaning* (Boston: Beacon, 1959), 66.
10. A Great Hope Fell," *The Complete Poems of Emily Dickinson,* edited by Thomas H. Johnson (Boston: Little, Brown and Co., 1960), no. 1123, 504-505.
11. Henri J. M. Nouwen, *The Wounded Healer* (New York: Doubleday, 1979), 88.
12. Ibid., 99-100. See also Gregory of Nyssa, exploring the image from the Song of Songs in which the bride says, "I am wounded with love": "Indeed it is a good wound and a sweet pain by which life penetrates the soul; for by the tearing of the arrow she opens, as it were, a door, an entrance into herself." In "Commentary on the Canticle," sermon 4, PG 44, 852A-853A, quoted in *From Glory to Glory: Texts from Gregory of Nyssa's Mystical Writings* (trans. and ed. Herbert Musurillo; New York: Charles Scribner's Sons, 1961), 179.
13. Father Edmundo Rodrigues, S.J., then director of Jesuit Spirituality Center, Grand Coteau, Louisiana.
14. Evagrius, *De Oratione,* PG 79, no. 5, 1168D, quoted by George Maloney, *Inward Stillness* (Denville, N.J.: Dimensions Books, 1976), 111.
15. Maloney, *Inward Stillness,* 105.
16. *De Beatitudine,* 111, PG 44, 1224C, quoted in Maloney, *Inward Stillness,* 113.
17. C. S. Lewis, *The Magician's Nephew* (New York: Macmillan, 1970), 142.
18. Ibid., 164.

Chapter 13: No Greater Love

1. Kenneth Leech, *Soul Friend* (London: Sheldon Press, 1977).
2. Kenneth Leech, "Is Spiritual Direction Losing Its Bearings?" *The Tablet,* 22 May 1993: 643.
3. Margaret Guenther, *Holy Listening: The Art of Spiritual Direction* (Boston: Cowley Publications, 1992).
4. Kathleen Fischer, *Women at the Well: Feminist Perspectives in Spiritual Direction* (New York: Paulist Press, 1988).
5. Aelred of Rievaulx, *Spiritual Friendship* (trans. Mary Eugenia

Laker; Kalamazoo, Mich.: Cistercian Publications, 1977).

6. Ibid., I:69.
7. Ibid., I:8.
8. Thomas à Kempis, *The Imitation of Christ*, trans. Leo Sherley-Price (London: Penguin Books, 1952), 148.
9. Aelred, *Spiritual Friendship,* II:15.
10. Ibid., II:49.
11. Ibid., II:11.
12. Ibid., I:37.
13. Ibid., III:6.
14. Ibid., I:21.
15. Ibid., III:104.
16. Not that Aelred himself was unaware of these perils of false friendship either in the world or in the monastery; see Aelred, *Spiritual Friendship,* I:60 and II:57.
17. The Book of Common Prayer (New York: Church Hymnal Corp., 1979), 355.
18. Aelred, *Spiritual Friendship,* I:1.
19. Alan Jones, *Exploring Spiritual Direction: An Essay on Christian Friendship* (San Francisco: Harper, 1982), 129.
20. Ibid., 127.
21. Aelred, *Spiritual Friendship,* III:104.
22. Ibid., III:10.
23. Robert J. McAllister, *Living the Vows* (San Francisco: Harper and Row, 1986), 225; quoted in Maggie Ross, "The Human Experience of God at Turning Points," *On Pilgrimage* (Toronto: Peregrina, 1994), 449.
24. Aelred, *Spiritual Friendship,* III:109.
25. Ibid., III:113.
26. See 2 Samuel 12:1ff.
27. Aelred, *Spiritual Friendship,* II:12.
28. Aelred of Rievaulx, *Mirror of Charity,* I:79 (emphasis added).
29. See Luke 24:13-35.
30. Ecclesiasticus 6:14-15.
31. Guenther, *Holy Listening,* 46-47.

32. Lyndall Gordon, *Eliot's New Life* (Oxford: Oxford University Press, 1988), 199. This thoughtful biography of T. S. Eliot is also a fascinating account of the role of friendship in a Christian life.
33. Thomas Kelly, *A Testament of Devotion* (New York: Harper & Brothers, 1941), 80, 82.
34. Ibid., 85.
35. Ibid., 86.
36. Ibid., 86–87.

Chapter 16: Of Woodstoves, Burnout, and the Living Flame of Love

1. Teresa of Avila, *The Book of Her Life,* in *The Collected Works of St. Teresa of Avila,* vol. 1 (trans. Kieran Kavanaugh and Otilio Rodrigues; Washington, D.C.: ICS Publications, 1987), chap. 15, para. 7. Later references to chapter and paragraph will be indicated by the number of each one, e.g., 15.7.
2. John of the Cross, *The Poems of St. John of the Cross* (trans. and intro. Willis Barnstone; New York: New Directions Press, 1972), 56.
3. Teresa of Avila, *The Way of Perfection,* in *The Collected Works of St. Teresa of Avila,* vol. 2 (trans. Kieran Kavanaugh and Otilio Rodrigues; Washington, D.C.: ICS Publications, 1980), chap. 28, para. 8.
4. Teresa of Avila, *The Book of Her Life,* 37.7.
5. Ibid., 39.23.
6. Ibid., 30.20.
7. Ibid., 30.21.
8. Ibid., 30.20.
9. Ibid., 37.7
10. “Prayer for the Care of Children,” in The Book of Common Prayer (New York: Church Hymnal Corp., 1979), 829.
11. *The Desert Christian: The Sayings of the Desert Fathers* (trans. Benedicta Ward; New York: Macmillan, 1975), 230.
12. Simone Weil, *Waiting for God* (trans. Emma Craufurd; New York: Harper Colophon, 1973), 210.
13. John of the Cross, *Poems of St. John,* 56.
14. Ibid.
15. Teresa of Avila, *The Book of Her Life,* 34.15

Chapter 17: Sparks Among the Stubble

1. *The Gospel According to Thomas* (Coptic text established and trans. A. Guillaumont et al.; New York: Harper & Row, 1959), Logia 82, p. 45.
2. Wisdom of Solomon 3:7.
3. *Book of Confessions,* pt. 1 of *The Constitution of the Presbyterian Church (U.S.A.)* (Louisville, Ky.: Office of the General Assembly, 1991), 10.1.
4. Edward Mote, "My Hope Is Built on Nothing Less," *The Church Hymnary* (Oxford: Oxford University Press, 1973), no. 411, p. 149.
5. Gerard Manley Hopkins, "God's Grandeur," in *Poems and Prose Selected and Edited by W. H. Gardner* (New York: Viking Penguin, 1953), 27.

Chapter 18: Vine and Branches

1. Henri J. M. Nouwen, *In the Name of Jesus: Reflections on Christian Leadership* (New York: Crossroad, 1992), 71.
2. Henri J. M. Nouwen, *Creative Ministry* (New York: Image Books, 1978), 87.
3. Teresa Benedicta of the Cross, quoted in Waltraud Herbstrith, *Edith Stein* (San Francisco: Harper & Row, 1971), 41.
4. Julius Marcus of Cologne, quoted in Herbstrith, *Edith Stein,* 105.
5. Report of Mr. Wielek in *De Tijd,* quoted in Herbstrith, *Edith Stein,* 107-8.
6. Henri J. M. Nouwen, *In the Name of Jesus,* 24.
7. Ibid., 28, 31-32.
8. Rainer Maria Rilke, "Just as the watchman in the wine fields," in *Selected Poems of Rainer Maria Rilke: A Translation from the German and Commentary* (trans. Robert Bly; New York: Harper & Row, 1982), 45. Prohibitive copyright restrictions prevent its being printed here in full.
9. Dylan Thomas, "The force that through the green fuse drives the flower," in *The Collected Works of Dylan Thomas* (New York: New Directions, 1971), 10.

Source Notes

The essays and poems in this volume previously appeared in a variety of periodicals. Following is a list of their original places of publication.

1. "Be of Few Words: Her Majesty's War on Verbosity" (*Commonweal*, vol. CXX, no. 22, 17 December 1993).
2. "How I Pray Now: Sometimes, No Words At All" (*New Covenant* 24, no. 5, December 1994).
3. "New Wine: Praying the Scriptures" (*Weavings* XI, no. 4, July/August 1996).
4. "To See with the Eyes of the Heart" (*Weavings* XII, no. 1, January/February 1997).
5. "Becoming Like Children" (*New Covenant* 22:6, January 1993).
6. "The Examen Reexamined" (*Weavings* X:2, March/April 1995).
7. "Touched by God" (*The Other Side* 33:2, Winter 1994).
8. "Nursing Home Visit" (*Daughters of Sarah* 20:1, Winter 1994).
9. "Broken Pieces: in the Fractioning We Are Made Whole" (*Commonweal* CXVIII: 9, 3 May 1991).
10. "Do You Want To Be Healed?" (*Weavings* VIII: 5, September/October 1995).
11. "Wounded and Healed" (*Weavings* XV: 2, March/April 2000).
12. "Grief on Ice" (*Weavings* VIII: 5, September/October 1993).
13. "No Greater Love: Reclaiming Christian Friendship" (*The Way* 35:1, January 1995).

14. "Between Friends" (*Emmanuel* 100:7, September 1994).
15. "Angels" (*Sacred Journey* 8:6, December 1997).
16. "Of Woodstoves, Burnout, and the Living Flame of Love" (*Spiritual Life* 40:3, Fall 1994).
17. "Sparks Among the Stubble: You Can Catch Fire" (*Horizons* 8:1, January/February 1995).
18. "Vine and Branches: Abiding in Christ" (*Weavings* XVI: 5, September/October 2001).
19. "Ash Wednesday" (*Emmanuel* 96:2, March 1990).